ISBN 978-1-330-95434-8
PIBN 10125905

This book is a reproduction of an important historical work. Forgotten Books uses
state-of-the-art technology to digitally reconstruct the work, preserving the original format
whilst repairing imperfections present in the aged copy. In rare cases, an imperfection in
the original, such as a blemish or missing page, may be replicated in our edition. We do,
however, repair the vast majority of imperfections successfully; any imperfections that
remain are intentionally left to preserve the state of such historical works.

1 MONTH OF
FREE
READING

at
www.ForgottenBooks.com

By purchasing this book you are eligible for one month membership to ForgottenBooks.com, giving you unlimited access to our entire collection of over 700,000 titles via our web site and mobile apps.

To claim your free month visit: www.forgottenbooks.com/free125905

English
Français
Deutsche
Italiano
Español
Português

www.forgottenbooks.com

Mythology Photography **Fiction**
Fishing Christianity **Art** Cooking
Essays Buddhism Freemasonry
Medicine **Biology** Music **Ancient**
Egypt Evolution Carpentry Physics
Dance Geology **Mathematics** Fitness
Shakespeare **Folklore** Yoga Marketing
Confidence Immortality Biographies
Poetry **Psychology** Witchcraft
Electronics Chemistry History **Law**
Accounting **Philosophy** Anthropology
Alchemy Drama Quantum Mechanics
Atheism Sexual Health **Ancient History**
Entrepreneurship Languages Sport
Paleontology Needlework Islam
Metaphysics Investment Archaeology
Parenting Statistics Criminology
Motivational

Poems of the Middle West

BY

WARREN BENTLEY GREGG

CEDAR RAPIDS, IOWA:
T. S. METCALF, Printer and Binder.
1899.

CONTENTS.

PREFACE.

A T the earnest request of many personal friends, I
have laid aside my own personal feelings of
seclusiveness and privacy in order to give this little
volume to the public.

It has been hastily written during the spare mo-
ments and hours that I have not been in the school-
room, and consequently may lack the finish that is
acquired in composition by those who have ample
time and opportunity for literary work.

In the hope that this book will meet the approval
of its readers, especially those who have asked for its
publication, it is respectfully submitted.

WARREN B. GREGG.

Anamosa, Iowa, March, 1899.

Poems of the "Middle West."

A SONNET.

O FRIENDS! to you these faulty lines I pen,
    To face the world, and meet the scoffs of men;
But you and all my fellow townsmen kind
Will not despise, tho' others faults may find.
Who condescends to men of station low,
Finds blessings rare around him freely flow;
As gentle music thrills and charms the soul
And onward in the distance seems to roll,
Then echoes back from a far away vale
The plaintive tones, with their rich golden tale;
So thine own unselfish deeds soon will come
And echo back kind favors one by one,
And golden tales of you that may be said,
Will live when you and I are silent, dead.

QUEEN OF THE MIDDLE WEST.

FAIR virgin queen, of our great Middle West!
      We love the natural charms of your face.
The robes of green that modestly enfold
Your graceful form in early spring, are like
Reception gowns of ancient fairy queens
Whose beauty did bewilder mortal eyes,
(Such as were favored with a blissful sight.)
The golden dress you wear in harvest time,
Displays the richness of your vast estates;
And all the lovers that throng 'round your feet,
Partake of hospitalities that're free.
Your features are not plain, but rounded here
And there; for 'tis in curves that beauty dwells
Without the stiffness of straight, formal lines.
And so, fair queen, presuming that you'll bear
With me, a humble subject of your realm,
If I relate the story of your birth,
Your noble parentage and childhood days;
I take my pen—forgiveness if I'm wrong!
But if you're pleased, then bless your native song.

Afar in western wilds where savage hordes
Did roam about in search of Bison droves;
Or, on account of some pretended wrong
Went forth in warpaint hideous, and with
Strange movements swift, peculiar to their tribe,
Went skulking on the unsuspecting foe
And feasted their revenge with cruelty; ·
A fertile region lay between two streams
Whose rushing torrents sped on to the sea
Quite unthought of, unnoticed, save by God
And fierce red men untutored in the law
Of Christian fellowship and civil arts;
Yet, having common laws that governed all
In tribal homes and in great councils, wars;
Displaying oft' sound wisdom, statesmanship,
And manners worthy of a noble race.
Rich pasturage was found o'er all this land;
And near its waters, forests did abound:
Thus nature seemed to give a special care
To this broad landscape stretching out so fair.

No plow had turned the soil to morning's sun;
For Anglo-Saxons here, were yet unknown;
Nor had the sturdy, German, immigrant

Found out the value of its farming land.
The missionaries of the French came first
To spread the gospel light and civil laws
Along the Mississippi's verdant banks.   ·
O, who will ever know what trials came
To those who braved the dangers that beset
On ev'ry side, our early pioneers? ·
They struggled on, the fathers of the West,
And faltered not, though oft' cast down with care:
New England and the Middle States sent forth
Their stalwart sons; and royal stock from far
Across the sea, gave to the Western Queen
Of states her righteous birth and guarded her
Till she became of age and gained a place
Among the stars that crown Columbia's brow.
Thus was the child conceived in love and born
In strength and might, while yet 'twas early morn!

Go to your aged grandsires whose gray locks
Have seen so many winters on the plains,
And learn of them how settlers strove to live,
To build their homes, and plant the corn for bread.
Dark Indian tales of frontier life are told
Of warriors slyly burning up the homes

And shooting down the inmates for revenge.
Our white-haired mothers can recall the time
When father drove his slow ox team to mill;
And she at home with children four or five
Oft' counted up the days when he'd return;
And hardly dared to think of what might be ·
If aught should harm the husband on the way.
The small brown huts in which the schools were kept
Turned out the future men who'd rise to fill
Responsible and honored positions high
In county, state, and national affairs;
Thus showing that instruction was not lost,
That hardy trials of those early days
Brought out the best of youth in many ways.

The founding of an empire state in peace
Is better than a hundred gained by war;
And conquerors armed well with axe and plow
Can do more good for all the human race
Than armies great with shining swords of steel.
'Tis education after all that makes
Our country free and great 'mong nations strong;
It gives the vital force to battle down
All discord and injustice that prevails.

The pioneers made haste to school the young,
They knew the strong inherent worth of books
And in their feeble strength did all they could
To foster and maintain the public schools.
And as their farms became a source of wealth,
They piled the funds for education high ;
And over all the land reared to the sun
Tall church-spires whose gilt tops portrayed
A beamy light of holiness to all
The country 'round where gospel light was felt
And lowly worshipers serenely knelt.

The ruralistic life of early homes
Whose curling smoke made ringlets in the air
And marked the distant huts of pioneers ;
Gave manhood, intellect, and self-control
To future generations of the plains.
In modest homes where sacred fires burn with
A cheerful glow throughout the years of life,
Are founded those pure sentiments from which
Just governments receive their fruitful source.
Yes, 'tis the love of home that binds our hearts
Together in one treasured spot on earth,
And turns our minds to that one blissful place

When sorrows come like evil birds of prey
To feast upon our hopes and bring despair.
Let's fan the fire that burns for love of home,
That keeps alive our history of old,
And makes a thrill of pride run through our veins;
Because our state is peaceful, wise, and great.
O, that the world would cease its constant strife
And cultivate a friendly, happy life!

Verse of tongue cannot express the sight
Of matchless fields with tasseled, yellow, corn
All waving in the balmy, healthful, air
And curing in the Autumn's potent sun:
Here, " Corn is king " and lacks no splendor grand,
But rules and sways the markets of the land.

What fellowship and love prevails in homes
Of western people of the hills and plains!
Where pure affections flow unstintedly,
As rivers timely fed by gushing springs.
So closely are the ties of friendship drawn
That love of country and of home is felt
Within the sturdy breasts of all our sons
Who dwell 'neath cottage roofs or slated halls.

And when our nation needs some fearless men
To vindicate her justice and defend
Her shores 'gainst evil plots of alien foes,
The West responds with energetic souls
Prepared to face cold death if it must be,
In order that Columbia may be free!

LEGEND OF HAWKEYE.

IN Mississippi's pleasant valley, long
   Ago, 'tis said there dwelt a warrior bold
Whose tow'ring strength did far outreach his tribe;
And all the chieftains west from Rockies came
To pay him tribute and to counsel 'bout
The things pertaining to great chiefs of might.
Oft' the incredulous came far to see
If half the stories of his wisdom could
Be founded on real truth unbiased, if
His hawk-like eyes did pierce their very thoughts
As oft' related by those coming from
His famous shrine of learning in the west.
Quite proud was he of all his warlike race;
For oft' he read on painted barks and skins
The story of his ancient fathers, their
First origin, their wanderings, and how
Across from Asia long ago, they steered
Through Behring Sea and found another shore
Created by the Great, Wise Spirit; for
His children of the earth to have a home.

Chief Hawkeye had ne'er crossed the muddy stream
Which lay just east of him; but oft' had heard
That charming queens of beauty ruled and swayed
The tribes whose land did stretch far out between
Great river systems of the North and West.
And eagerly inquiring of the chiefs
Who paid their yearly visits to his lodge
He learned of one, a Midland Queen, whose face
Was likened to the sun, so daz'ling fair;
And that the virgin maidens of her court
Did fascinate all strangers that came near.
At first, affecting that he little cared
To hear about this chaste and lovely one;
Pretended not to hear the praises said
In her behalf about her royal grace
Or of the lustre and magnificence
Displayed by all the beauties of her court.
Yet, somehow she would linger in his thoughts
And he'd be dreaming of the Midland Queen;
Nor could not stop, till he himself had seen.

Accordingly the brave young Hawkeye rose
And vowed he'd visit this bewitching maid
Known in the west afar as Midland Queen.

He called together all his chiefs and said:
" Make ready our canoes to journey east,
Select the strongest braves and deck them well
With paint and finery profusely placed;
Devise some queer maneuvers that will awe
And please the hostile strangers that we meet."
He gathered up the trinkets made of gold
Which western chiefs had fashioned out for him,
And many other things that squaws had made
To deck the Queen if she should worthy be.
His royal retinue indifferent
To fear or death, approved the chieftain's trip,
And gloried in the hope that trouble might
Ensue ere they returned, to give them fame
Among the older warriors left at home.
They crossed the rushing waters black and deep
And touched the shore where banks were high and
      steep.

The Midland Queen had heard of Hawkeye's fame
And secretly had hoped that fate ere long
Would bring this noble warrior of the plains
To her own land that she might see his face.
She pictured him as tall, with shoulders broad

And having graceful movements with his speech
And in his walk, a firm elastic tread;
His features seemed to be of finer mold
Than any warrior of her court and realm.
Ah, note the flashing of her eyes, the quick
Red tinging of her cheek when word is brought
By runners from the west, that Hawkeye with
A peaceful band is marching to the east.
The queen feigns illness, then at once retires
In order that she may have time alone
To think, and quell the throbbings of her heart;
For 'twould detract from dignity to see
A queen give way to sentimental thoughts,
And thus display a weakness of the pate
Before her court and ministers of state.

When Hawkeye with his warriors came in view,
Then all the queen's strong chieftains brave, with
          queer
Fantastic steps, advanced to pay respects
And welcome this proud ruler to their home.
And Hawkeye not to be outdone performed
The army tactics of his tribe, whose build
And manners much impressed the native men.

Then came the village maidens with gay songs
And graceful steps that marked the meter of
Their sylph-like motions in the dreamy dance;
And waving garlands of green leaves above
Their heads, commenced a ballad of their tribe
As they drew near, to greet the western king;
And thus the lyric ran:

WAUDINA.

Waudina was a happy maid
 And knew no care or harm;
She lived within the forest shade
 And felt no strange alarm.

There came a suitor for her hand
 And claimed he loved her well;
He told her of his native land
 Where she would like to dwell.

He promised all his life to love
 This handsome girl so fair;
And like a gentle cooing dove
 He won her unaware.

She left her father's pleasant home
  And gave her plighted vow;
That with this warrior young she'd roam
  And to his wishes bow.

Alas! how soon a heart can change!
  Waudina met her fate;
The husband's heart was cold and strange,
  All love had turned to hate.

Then brave Waudina in despair,
  Rushed for her father's land;
And left the other wives to share
  Her lover's cruel hand.

Waudina reached her native soil;
  But crossing o'er a stream
Where raging waters foam and boil,
  She seemed as in a dream:

She fell far down into the foam
  And never more was seen;
But now she comes to sigh and moan
  When spring floods wash the green.

LOVE.

O love is fickle and untrue!
  And maids are oft' deceived:
The ones that really love, are few,
  And they are not believed.

Some think they love, but fail to see
  That 'tis but surface deep;
While bleeding hearts must broken be
  And others lie in sleep.

You may not read a maiden's heart
  By outward signs and ways;
Nor know that love's own cruel dart,
  Has blasted all her days.

Chief Hawkeye seemed astonished at the scene
And listened quite intently to the song
Which so pathetically described the fate,
Waudina suffered through false words of love.
Next came the princely band of royal guards
To take his highness to their gracious queen:
And taking all the wisest men of war,
Proceeded to the palace with the guides.

The palace was surrounded by a grove
So dense, that nothing larger than a fox
Could pass within, except, by one straight road
That entered from the south and joined the square,
Wherein the Midland Queen kept up her court.

The trees along this road on either side,
Were thickly intertwined with ivy vines
That seemed to form a perfect wall of green
Far as the eye could see.   No weeds or brush
Defaced the highway here, but ev'rywhere
Rich meadow grass was growing in the sun
And songsters in the trees were never done.

The palace was built of gray limestone rock
And stood two stories high, a solid pile
Of massive stone reared up to face the sun.
The square was paved with river rock near by;
And shady trees with scented flowers lent
Delightful perfumes to the balmy air.
As Hawkeye neared the court, the drums beat out
The calls and warriors sallied forth to guard
Against surprise and intercept all but
The dignitaries that belonged to courts.

When Hawkeye and his retinue came near
The throne, the queen arose and bowed while all
Her faultless beauties of the brilliant court,
Arose and bowed with salutations grave.
Her majesty besought him to take seat
Beside the throne, and if 'twould please his grace,
The maidens of the palace would recite
Some noted epic of their ancient tribe
To liven up his spirits in some way
And make his visit here a pleasant stay.

WAPELLA*.

I.

[LEADER]

Wapella, prince of all his kin,
Possessed a fascinating way;
A gallant youth was he indeed
'Mong maidens of the leafy dell;
For many true hearts loved him well.

[CHORUS OF THE MAIDENS]

He was beloved by thoughtful men
Who gather knowledge when they can;

(*Wapella—The little prince.)

Adored for manly virtues known
By those who shared his lodge and home.

[LEADER]

He led the forces of his tribe
By speeches wise and timely said
When matters of importance came
Before the council of the chiefs;
His fiery eloquence was known
Throughout the land where it had flown.

II.

[CHORUS OF THE MAIDENS.]

O he could stir with magic art,
The sleeping music of the heart!
He knew the cords of tender ring
And often touched each gentle string!

[LEADER.]

And nature much assistance gave
This little prince of wondrous fame;
For he was fair as morning sky
When June's sun rises in the east:
His dark eye flashed with liquid fire
Inherit'd from his aged sire.

[CHORUS OF THE MAIDENS.]

He was a brilliant star of light
That shone far out into the night,
And lighted up with wisdom's rays
The lonely path where justice strays.

III.

[LEADER.]

He went away to forests deep
To find a maid both kind and true;
As gentle as a harmless doe
And lovely as a fairy nymph;
One that he'd love and cherish long
And one that bards would bless with song.

[CHORUS OF THE MAIDENS.]

He went to seek the sweetest bird
That ever mortal soul had heard
Or seen within the shady trees
Fann'd by the purest zephyr breeze.

[LEADER.]

Wapella stole upon a tribe
And found the beauty of his choice;

The artful maids retired from view,
Pretended that he frightened them;
Just hid from sight, they danced and sang
Till with their songs, the forest rang.

IV.

[CHORUS OF THE MAIDENS.]

They moved about with lightest tread
Where're the leading singer led;
Assumed to be quite hid from view,
As timid maids are apt to do.

[LEADER.]

He asked the chieftain for her hand,
But he raved fiercely at the prince
And bade him leave ere morning sun;
For he would never give away
His daughter to a foreign prince;
And arguments would not convince.

[CHORUS OF THE MAIDENS.]

O, hateful father, cease your ire
And let those wed who so desire!
Let arguments your mind convince;
For he's a charming little prince!

V.

[LEADER.]

Wapella waved a kind adieu,
But straightway found the maiden true
And they two fled in evening dew;
Nor did the maiden ever rue
Her flight 'way with the charming prince.
When arguments would not convince.

[CHORUS OF THE MAIDENS.]

O sing!   ye fairies of the dell;
The chieftain's lost his forest belle!
She fled 'way with the noble prince
When arguments would not convince!

Amidst the grandeur and enthusiasm
Prevalent at the ceremonies here,
Chief Hawkeye could think only of the queen
Whose elegance did far surpass his most
Expectant dreams of what she'd likely be:
He made a firm resolve to win her hand
Or die; for he could never live without
This fairy nymph to grace his lodge and home.

And she oft' glanced at his wise, noble face
When he intently seemed to look across
The room at some maneuver of the maids
Who danced about and sang their lyric songs.
Yes, she loved him with zealous heart and soul;
And said within herself, " I'll gain this chief,
Or else live on, unmated and alone."
Just then, the war drums beat the warriors' charge!
An awful warning that fierce blood ran wild!
The war whoops of the palace guards rang out,
Like demons thirsting for revenge and gore;
They waved their gleaming spears 'mid frantic roar!

The rash young warriors from the distant West
Had picked a quarrel with the native chiefs
On purpose for renown and fame when they
Returned among the chieftains of their homes.
So when the armies gave the war-whoop yell,
The palace guards surrounded in the square
The foreign warriors and began to dance,
And menace with their spears the haughty heads
Of Hawkeye's western braves. While some led off
To find the royal visitor and bring
Him out to see his warrors humbled low.

The queen refused them passage through the door;
Then ordered all the guards to cease, retire,
And show respect for strangers at her court.
Meanwhile, the tide of battle turned, and with
A mighty yell the troops of Hawkeye came
In overwhelming force, and reached the square
Wherein the palace stood, and blind with rage, ·
Made for the throne-room door to kill the queen;
But Hawkeye stood and formed a perfect screen.

Then Hawkeye reprimanded his fierce chiefs
And sent away the leaders in disgrace.
When order in the square had been restored,
'Twas found the queen's chief counselor was dead;
The aged father of her noble tribe,
Brave Kokowah, the minister of state.
Soon all the maidens of the court and tribe
Began to wail the mourning hymn used when
Some member of the household passed away.

MOURNING HYMN.

Oh! desolate are all our hearts,
 Our eyes with tears are damp;

We mourn in sorrow for the dead,
  As 'round his bier we tramp.

Oh! we must bear this awful woe
  And trouble for his sake;
Because we loved his manly heart
  And did his friendship take.

Oh! strange indeed, that he should die,
  The one we all adored;
And leave us here to mourn his loss
  Without our hearts restored.

Now, lonely ones of earth are we;
  Our friend is stiff and cold
And all the merry songs have ceased;
  For death doth now enfold.

A pit was dug within the grove wherein
Five men could stand; the sides were deftly lined
With native rock found near the river beds;
And on the bottom, robes and furs were placed;
That he might have a pleasant sleep and rest,
While waiting for the happy, hunting grounds
His ancient fathers would some day possess.

They placed him sitting up within his grave;
And 'round about him stored his ornaments,
With many bows and arrows of his make
And sharpened knives to dress what game he'd take.
The queen with dignity, 'mid solemn looks
And tears, proceeded to the pit where sat
The dead chief, Kokowah, and listened to
A famous orator, Chief Keokuk,
"The Watchful Fox," for such his name implied.

ORATION OF KEOKUK.

O! fathers of my tribe, what shall I say
To comfort and assuage this grief of ours?
Can words of mine portray the sorrow which
The nation feels now weighing at its heart?
O that my sight had faded ere I saw
The death of Kokowah, our mighty chief!
Who'll take his place to counsel and advise
Our queen and warriors on the battlefield?
Oh, Kokowah! wake up and speak again!
It must not be that Kokowah is dead!

The birds will come again to sing each spring,
The trees will bud and blossom in the sun;

And all the land in ecstacy will sing
But our dead chieftain will return no more.
Can eloquence depict or celebrate
The justice in a perfect man of earth?

The nearer that men reach to perfect ways,
The harder 'tis for orators to sing their praise;
For language signs cannot express the light
Within a person that is doing right.
O that my tongue could by so some magic art
Reveal to you the life-work of this chief!
He planned our lodges and this verdant grove,
And built yon palace for our maiden queen;
He trained the life guards of our royal court;
Invented drills and signs to use in war,
And led to victory our valliant braves.
Oh, warriors! is he sleeping yet?   Alas!
His last long resting place is finished, done,
And he will view no more the rising sun!
Not many moons have passed since Kokowah
Led out the warriors to defend our land
Against insatiate hordes that came here
To burn our wigwams and to take away .
Our wives and children to be wretched slaves!

All unexpectedly we raised the cry
Known only when incensed braves of our tribe, ,
Go out to drive invaders from our soil !
Oh ! how the maidens danced when Kokowah,
Returned from battle with his braves, and stood
Before the queen, to tell her that the foes
Who were not dead, had fled beyond pursuit.
Impetuous young warriors hear these words :
Chief Kokowah weighed carefully the cause
And probable results of ev'ry war ;
He counseled peace when 'twould protect
His people and their fathers' graves from harm.
But if the plotting chiefs of other tribes
Encroached upon our native grounds to kill,
Then Kokowah fought with an iron will !

Belov'd, he was not faithless in his home ;
Nor lacking wisdom and precaution, which
Are needful when confirming laws of state
Or dealing with those cunning chiefs outside
The bound'ries of our native streams and hills.
Do not misunderstand my purpose braves,
If my encomium should seem devoid
Of feeling, when I say, that Kokowah

Had many serious faults; for he was
An earthly chieftain, and quite liable
To errors of the head, because of things
Beyond his sight and far from his control.
I know that certain vulgar orators
Are prone to work for men's insensate praise;
And seeming to be eulogizing, oft'
Instead, are making use of glaring lies,
Quite plain to those who calmly weigh their words
In justice's scales, and thus obtain the truth.
O, warriors of the plains, be great and wise!
For in false words, much of our trouble lies.

'Twill be of little value now to us
To fill our minds with past and sad regrets;
So let us think of future problems which
Will come to tax the wisdom of our chiefs.
O, friends, and brothers! study well your plans
And gather with the wisest of your men,
For counsel and advice. Invite the chiefs
From other tribes to meet in peaceful bands;
And settle their disputes with friendly words,
Without the horrors of these bloody wars.
Oh, warriors! there is much that's not in war!

And peaceful pleasures are more lasting in
Results.   So, till the virgin soil beneath
Your feet, and build a palace for each home!
Then will the rosy morn dawn on your hopes;
Your fields bring forth abundant grains and roots;
And like the happy hunting grounds, much game
Will feed upon your plains and in your groves.
Give way to peace, braves of the Midland sun!
Attend your dead; for Keokuk is done!

When Keokuk had ended, and the pit
Was covered o'er with slabs of heavy rock,
The warriors sang a mournful requiem
And raised a mound of earth up o'er the grave.
Immediately to the palace came
The braves distinguished for their size and strength,
To hear the orders from the throne and learn
What lucky chief should counsel with the queen.
Queen Lomana, with modest etiquette,
Arose and led the gallant Hawkeye out
Where all could see his manly form and face;
And in a clear and mellow voice declared,
That Hawkeye was to be her counselor,
And all their people must unite in peace.

The warriors bowed, and gay the maidens sang;
While peaceful fires illumed the fragrant air.
The king and queen went out to view the land
And when he saw the rivers and the hills
He then enthusiastically exclaimed:
" Fair Iowa, the beautiful!"

THE ORATION OF NANAMAKEE*

WARRIORS! arouse! and take no sleep!
  You are not puny babes!   Awake!
Does not your fathers' blood cry out
For justice and redress?   Must squaws
Put on the paint and fight the Sioux,
While you recline in ease at home?
Are you afraid to face the northern foe
That those invaders rest upon our soil?

Do brave Sac warriors ever count the cost,
Or shrink from petty foes in shame?
Your long delay has stirred the bones
Of aged warriors in their graves!
Are there no braves still left to fight?
Why then, do you put off this war?
Have you not heard the older chiefs
Relate the prowess of our tribe
And show the scalps of many Sioux?

Think of the wigwams which were burned!
The fields of corn despoiled by them;

*Na-na-ma-kee (The Thunderer). Grandfather of Black Hawk.

While we were journeying from home
In search of game for winter use.
The Sac must not forget this wrong,
Till ev'ry foe has left our groves!
Why do you wait?   Prepare for war!
Call up the braves and deck with paint!

Begin the scalp dance, men of war!
The spirits of our chiefs are here!
List to the ancient war-whoop of
Your fathers leading on the dance!
The medicine men have told the chiefs
That many scalps will grace the belts
Of all our warriors who will go!

THE LAMENT FOR OTTUMWANO*

THE white men from the east have come
    And taken all our hunting grounds;
They've given but a paltry sum
    For all this land where game abounds.

We shall not see each pleasant glen;
    Our native chiefs must no more roam
The plains and hills, or see again
    Ottumwano, that was our home!

The red men soon will be forgot,
    Like autumn leaves drove by the breeze
To dwell in some obscure, lone spot,
    Away from all the mother trees.

Our fathers' tears did not avail
    To stay the white man's coming here;
And so our people moan and wail;
    Ottumwano must disappear!

*Ot-tum-wa-no, now called Ottumwa.
    When the time for leaving Ottumwano arrived, a solemn silence
prevailed in the Indian camp, and the faces of their stoutest men
were bathed in tears; and when their cavalcade was put in motion,
toward the setting sun, there was a spontaneous outburst of frantic
grief from the entire procession.—History of Iowa.

For us, the sun has no bright dawn ;
  We've but one weary, cloudy day ;
Our village and our homes are gone ;
  They've come to send us far away !

The great High Spirit knows how we
  Were forced to sell our fathers' land !
The white man gave a money fee
  And pointed westward with the hand.

O, warriors, cease your weeping now !
  'Tis done and past beyond recall ;
And o'er your dead, the white man's plow
  Will turn the sod in spring and fall.

Array the braves of war once more
  As for a conflict with a foe !
For struggles of the heart wax sore,
  And love of home brings back our woe !

A solemn hush stole o'er the camp
  When all the tribe prepared to go ;
And stoutest warriors' eyes were damp
  With tears that did not cease to flow.

They started west 'mid woeful sighs
　　And painful thoughts that filled each mind;
They went with mournful tears and cries;
　　Ottumwano was left behind!

Oh, how they strove to beat it back!
　　That overwhelming flood of grief!
Which swept along their lonely track
　　And tore their hearts without relief!

The people moved as in a trance;
　　But turning once, they raised a cry:
"Oh! let us give one parting glance!
　　Ottumwano! good-bye! good-bye!"

SONG TO THE MORNING.

I.

O birds, wake up and sing your lays
   Without a sign of fear !
For now, in all rich splendor bright,
   Gay morning doth appear.
She's rested through the hazy night;
   Her sleep was calm, secure,
But now awakes when daylight breaks,
   With garments clean and pure.

II.

The morning's breath, so sweet, gives life
   And vigor unto all,
And hastens on the busy feet
   To duty's urgent call:
She sits a queen in fairest robes
   And rules the early hour;
As a maiden fair in looks and worth,
   Doth sway with gentle power.

III.

Still strong and young the morning stays,
  No wrinkles on the brow ;
While 'bout her throne on ev'ry side,
  The aged world must bow:
O, sing to one whose beaming smile
  Is always on her face!
The morning hour in beauty fair,
  That shows such charming grace.

THE PENITENTIARY.

WHY are thy massive walls reared high in air
      And on their tops, men watching with such
   care?
What mean these pillars strong of solid stone,
Those swinging doors of steel that screech and groan?
Is there a foe without that seeks thy harm?
Ah, no! 'tis foes within that do alarm:
Just like the human heart where doth abide
Fierce envy, wrath, presumptuous sin and pride:
These all must be restrained by strong, firm hands
That are joined kindly by love's Christian bands,
And thus lead back the erring from his way,
Back to bright hopes, good deeds, a happy day:
For sinful man may not fall down so low
That the omnipotent God cannot go
To raise him once again in mercy's name
And cleanse his aching heart from sin and shame.

THE COLLEGE BRIDGE.

IN memory's rich urn I'll leave a place
   In which I may in after years retrace
My steps once more across the dear old bridge
That spans the track from the hillside ridge,
And see again those friends of by-gone days
Who used to light us up in many ways
With pleasant looks, and cheerful, happy words
From kind, good hearts free as the singing birds.
Delightful spot in which to breathe the air,
No place has half the charms or is so fair
To those who must a recreation seek,
After the long hard studies of the week.
Fast trains that glide so quickly underneath,
Send steam and smoke in a long winding wreath
High up above to meet the azure sky
As onward east and west they swiftly fly.
The well-worn boards which form the floor and walk,
Could tell many a tale if they could talk,
Of friendships formed that life-long lasted,
Of fondest hopes that were ruined, blasted.
Ah, shall I e'er forget my schoolmates dear,
Ne'er send a wreath nor drop a silent tear ;

When they have ended their short, earthly race
And no more fill their long accustomed place?
Oh, no! I cry: Return, return, sweet past!
If thou art gone, no future joys can last!
The present day with all its cares and woes,
Will brighter get by mem'ry's radiant glows.

MARY.

IN a rich state, where great trees wave in air
  And crystal lakes and rivers everywhere—
Seem to be vieing with the flowers near,
With singing birds, whose notes are sweet and clear,
To put to shame the artist's feeble art
By painting living pictures of the heart:
Here are seen pleasant homes on fertile farms
Where dwells the farmer, whose strong brawny arms
Cut down the forest in an early day,
And made a home where loved ones all might stay.
Here, when the state was young, the woods were
    dense,
'Most everybody had a long rail fence.
'Tis said, the wolf and bear made nightly calls
On helpless sheep and cattle in their stalls,
And that the deer would feed and sport near by,
While busy farmers sowed their wheat and rye.

II.

There came to this state in an early time,
A man and wife, in vigor, youth and prime:

They brought three children with them here,
To bless their home—fond little ones, so dear.
He was impetuous, yet smart and brave
And made good money, but he could not save;
For when it seemed that all was doing well
He ceased his work and tried to trade or sell ;
Yet, nevertheless, till past middle life, .
He still had plenty, (thanks to his good wife).
His wife was calm, she weighed her actions well,
And what she said, or did, was sure to tell :
She seldom crossed her husband in his way
But patiently looked forward to a day
When a good, happy home would be their lot,
Where care and strife should trouble not.

III.

This wife was fair and noble, yet not vain,
But kind, sincere and true—Mary was her name.
The proud. rich blood of her ancestral race
Was plainly visible in that calm face.
She had great pride, but showed it not in ways
That would attention draw to public gaze ;
But in her modest home she took great care

To keep it pure and wholesome everywhere.
Her children early learned the way to go
In which to shun the idle and the low;
Because she never counseled aught but peace,
Fierce strife was stopped and anger soon would cease;
Like flames that suddenly burst out and roar,
But soon die out and then are seen no more,
For lack of material on which to feed
Their craving appetite and wicked greed.

IV.

O, blessed are those saintly ones of earth,
Whose lives of purity and perfect worth
Do lead the sinful heart to seek its God
And follow ways that angels bright have trod!
O, who shall count that truly glorious band
Who'll stand for God, led by a loving hand?
Some ideal life, lived over day by day,
Hath turned many a sinner from his way:
These living sermons not from printed scroll,
Are those that touch the heart and win the soul.
Like fresh, cool fountains in a lonely place,
Found by the hunter in the long, hard chase—

So are kind deeds, when we are sick with care
And life's fond hopes are gone, we know not where.
O, dear, kind hands, your loving earnest deeds
Are far more righteous than our long church creeds.

v.

Time went on, and the Wolverine Lake state
Grew up with all her sisters, rich and great;
And when our country saw its darkest day,
Her sons marched forth in grand array
To duty's call, that said: " Defend your flag
And never let your efforts halt or lag,
Till armed resistance shall all cease to be
And our proud Ensign waves from sea to sea."
Right well they served, and then came home at last;
The war had ceased; still was the cannon's blast.
A grateful nation sang their praise and worth,
And blessed the happy land that gave them birth:
The "Union of States" at last prevailed;
No more would the old Flag be assailed;
But peace and happiness would be the lot
In a land where fierce woes are soon forgot.

VI.

While war was raging, great was Mary's faith
That God would aid, that freedom would be safe.
She often said to her despairing friends:
" God's ways are right and lead to joyful ends."
Before the war two children joined the flock,
Just five in all that Mary had to rock.
The oldest daughter was married and away
Before the youngest saw her first birthday.
As years rolled on, grandchildren blessed the home,
Where Mary and her husband lived alone;
With their innocent prattle, mirth and fun,
The hearts of the old folks they fairly won.
Thus Mary seemed to live her young days o'er
With her grandchildren playing 'round the door,
Or perhaps sitting on grandfather's knee,
He told them stories while they laughed with glee.

VII.

There came a day (that day comes to us all),
When Mary answered the " Death Angel's call."
Ah, then came bitter tears of sad regret,
From those who oft their duty did forget,

When patient mother still worked hard at home,
Quite unthought-of, neglected and alone.
O, for one passing hour in which to say :
" Dear mother, forgive us, and for us pray ! "
But no, not till the " resurrection morn "
Can a loving message to her be borne.
O, that good deeds were done and kind words said
While yet our friends could know—before they're
    dead !
Now Mary sleeps unmindful of her cares,
Untempted by deceiving, worldly snares ;
Truth was her motto, peace was her dream,
The Bible she loved, for 'twas her theme.

"DRIFTED IN."

I.

STRANGE are experiences that often come
To harass, to perplex, or frighten one!
To you, fair teachers, I wish to recall
A winter's day, familiar to you all.
The sun came up, but showed a chilly face,
As if he saw the storm in its mad chase
And knew how queer and strange would be the
plight
Of many blithsome hearts ere the fall of night.

II.

With minds quite heedless of the direful storm
And wrapped in furs and robes, so snug and warm,
A merry crowd of workers on that day
Were going to a meeting—strange to say
Their thoughts did wander oft from sad to gay,
And discussions changed 'round most ev'ry way,
Like thistle down when it floats here and there,
Directed by the motion of the air.

III.

The cold, white snow came drifting down quite fast
Accompanied by the wind's chilling blast;
And as the day wore on, the storm grew fierce,
Through ev'ry wrap and cover seemed to pierce;
And whirling off the snow from ev'ry hill,
It piled the roads with drifts, which lay quite still;
While thick dark clouds brought on the dreary night
Like shutters closed at early candle light.

IV.

An inward dread came o'er most ev'ry one,
Which caused a slacking of the mirth and fun;
For silent thoughts of what the end might be
Filled many a heart, and stopped all cheerful glee.
Yet, some kept up an optimistic show
And cheered the others with their warmth and glow;
As doctors strengthen those sick and in bed
By cheerful looks, and bright words which are said.

V.

But faster fell the cutting, icy hail
And loudly whistled the mad, roaring gale;

The horses struggled on, as well they tried
To overcome the drifts on ev'ry side.
Soon all trace of the road was lost to view:
"We're Drifted In," said all the helpless crew.
The poor steeds turned their heads as if to see
If there was hope, or what their fate would be.

VI.

Some crawled about the teams in drifts waist-deep,
Expecting in the snow that night to sleep;
But a cry was raised 'midst the storm so cold:
"See! yonder shines a light! the house will hold
Us all: Let's go, no matter what the fees;
'Tis better than staying out here to freeze."
And so around the country fireside bright,
They told of trips and jokes—far in the night.

VII.

And when they could no longer keep awake,
Tho' friendly hands gave drowsy heads a shake,
They fell asleep and dreamed of early dawn,
That when the morning came the snow was gone,
And happy birds were singing in a grove:

A long, deep snore—a stir—too near the stove!
The morning came and soon awoke each one:
The storm was o'er ; bright was the cheering sun.

PART SECOND.

VIII.

There are ways in which we might be " Drifted In "
By public sentiment's fast waving din
O'ertaking us in fault quite unaware,
And hauling down our castles from the air:
Our hopes of progress and of future pay
All " Drifted In," lost forever by the way ;
For when the people take your case in hand,
Then only true and loyal ones can stand.

IX.

We've often " Drifted In " by storms of doubt,
Assailed by theories false that stalk about
And covered up by banks of error high ;
While reason fails, unable to pass by
Where bold audacious schemes benight the way
And hide the common sense of our own day,
That otherwise might guide us on afar
And cause our work to move without a jar.

X.

Most ev'ry year great changes come about,
We may drift in where some have drifted out:
The earnest teacher who has toiled with care,
Will be thought of, remembered ev'rywhere.
And when in death we rest, so cold and still,
With all our faults and erring ways, it will
Be said—we've battled well against all sin
And won the Crown—and not just " Drifted In."

Read at the County Association of Teachers, held at Anamosa,
Iowa, May 7, 1898.

DEWEY.

HURRAH for Dewey! and our sailors at sea!
  Rejoice, O America, land of the free!
Hurrah, for the wonderful victory!
In books of golden deeds their names will stand
And songs of praise ring out on sea and land
Commemorating this valiant fight so brave
Where the defeated foe found a wat'ry grave.
Our sailors have avenged with cannon's roar
The blood of those who died near Cuba's shore:
'Twas Dewey's fleet that sailed to meet the foe;
He gave the word that let the great guns go;
He set on fire and tore the hostile fleet
In fragments small, it strewed the deep;
Its burning cinders rose up in the air
And left Spain's admiral in despair.

O, Dewey! you're the ideal man
  That's brought " Old Glory" back
To shine once more as in days of yore
  Upon the ocean track.
Yes, they shall know o'er all the world
  Where'er our Ensign floats,
That America has noble men
  In mighty ocean boats!

DON'T FORGET ME.

DON'T forget me!
　　In the walk of busy life,
'Mid the trial and confusion
In this constant world of strife.

　　Don't forget me!
When with troubles you are sad,
　　Discontented and down-hearted,
Trust your friend, he'll make you glad.

　　Don't forget me!
When I'm far away from you,
　　I am just as kind and faithful
And my heart beats just as true.

　　Don't forget me!
When you come to Heaven's gate,
　　Knock gently for admission,
Just inside for you I'll wait.

MUSIC.

IT is grand music which imparts
　The inward feelings of our hearts:
That gift from God, so good, sublime,
A blessing for man throughout all time.

To David, ancient singer of old,
God made a promise and foretold,
That His throne should always stand
And His son rule o'er all the land.

When the glad news to earth was giv'n
That Christ was born and sent from Heav'n,
The angels sang in chorus grand
To shepherds in the holy land.

When Jesus knew his work was done,
A final hymn alone they sung,
And then with his disciples by,
Went forth for you and me to die.

I hold that music's most divine
That strikes the tender cords of love,
When purest thoughts control the soul
And turn the mind to God above.

SPEAK FROM THE HEART.

SPEAK not from the written page,
  Thoughts purposely acquired ;
Speak from the inner soul
  The things the heart inspires.

Indulge not in idle tales
  That inwardly are false ;
Let not your mind go wandering
  Like maidens in a waltz.

The silly farce you're acting out,
  Is plain to those around you ;
Your hyperbole is much too large
  To float in such a narrow gorge.

Speak out the truth, cut where it may,
  And better always left unsaid
Deceitful things, to flatter ears
  That will forget you when you're dead.

Say pleasant words, but pass on by,
  Draw the curtains very close ;
Peep not out to apologize
  For having covered up a ghost.

THE LITTLE PINK.

O, little pink, that came so far!
    As precious as some dainty star;
Though but a humble little pink,
    What memories around you link!

When I planted you so far away,
    The heart was sad on that May day;
For grandma's grave you covered o'er,
    The grandma that the child will e'er adore.

And now, you've come to bless this state,
    Grow up and blossom at a rapid rate,
Cheering the poor, the sick, and sad;
    Making life better, with hearts that are glad.

SONG OF POETS.

BEAUTIFUL songs of the poets!
   Great thoughts of the ages rehearsed.
O, that expression complete,
   Could be giv'n the poets' sweet verse!
The lessons of truth and of duty,
   All told in the loveliest way;
Reminding the soul of the beauty
   That's hid in the life of today.

How our hearts throb wild with emotions!
   Some poet recites in his lines,
The wonderful deeds of the ages
   Which happened before our times.
The stories which are told by poets,
   Are things that men ought to hear;
For parts that will not do good,
   Are blotted with a silent tear.

Not half of the beauties of nature
   'Mid life's confusion and worry,
Would e'er be noticed or cherished

Without poets to write of their story.
Sing on, O poets of the nations!
    Your verses are grand and sublime!
You have taught a glorious lesson
    Our Creator is surely divine.

THE TEACHER'S GOOD-BYE.

THE endless chain has ceased to turn,
  There comes a time when tears will burn,
The routine work of many days
Must change about in different ways;
A long and needful rest—a wistful sigh,
We hail the closing hours—good-bye.

Yet, if again we turn not back
To work along the same old track,
May others greet us kindly, well,
Not heeding what to us befell
In bygone days.   Still loving good,
We'll do our duty as we should.

Like birds that're sheltered from the storm
When dark clouds roll and tempests warn,
So children dear in shelter save
When passions storm and vices rave.
Father, save them from tempting sin
That hence in glory they may win.

O, children, you who love me best!
Think well, when I am laid to rest:
Forget your idle words to say,
Forget this frail, poor, helpless clay;
Throw off your troubles like the birds,
But, Oh, do not forget my words!

GET THE THEME.

YOU should not say a book you've read
 Unless the theme's found in your head;
For he who reads and cannot tell
The moral, truth, or what befell
The characters within the book,
Might better never in it look.

Why wear the leaves and spoil the sides
To gratify your foolish eyes?
No use to weary by a constant grind,
Revolving words through an empty mind.

'Tis thoughts before the words are said
Should come from mind within your head :
So work away with steady thinking,
Your mind with greater ones keep linking,
And deem it wrong in jest or play
To treat good books in a careless way.

FLATTERY.

A KING is flattery o'er this earth,
  He rules men's actions from their birth :
When one dares to dissent from him,
His cause will suffer, 'tis hard to win.

How vain and foolish doth it appear
To flatter one while he is near !
Hypocrisy then reigns supreme,
And things are far from what they seem.

The truth is sure to be modified,
And those who flatter perhaps have lied,
When flattering words escape the tongue
To win some favor when they're done.

Kind words, fond hopes and wishes well,
Require no lies to express or tell ;
But flattery used to influence men,
With hateful words rebounds again.

TO A WOMAN WHO HAS WRITTEN A
WICKED NOVEL.

O, CREATURE of the dust, poor mortal clay!
    How will you face your God in judgment,
    say?
What answer will you give for all this wrong,
When you come up with all that countless throng?
You've lightly dealt with the word of your God
And followed evil paths which are not trod
By those who meekly strive to do what's right,
And be well pleasing in their Maker's sight.

Can anyone measure the fearful cost,
Or count the souls that harmful books have lost?
Your book may please some careless, wicked man;
Some idle boy or girl your lines may scan,
But all the noble men and women good
Will shun your book, and leave you as they should:
'Tis said that men are weak and bad, forlorn—
Why?   Because by women they were born.

There are grand women pure, with merry hearts
Whose ev'ry look sends love with cupid's darts:
With gentle words, quick wit, a winning way,
The hearts of gallant youths they capture, slay.
And mothers true, in whose sweet beaming face
No sign of wicked novels you can trace.
Oh! pray that more may be good mothers, dear,
Who'll bless the home and fireside all the year.

CHRISTMAS EVE

FROM

FIVE TO SEVENTY-FIVE.

DELIGHTFUL was the night when little Fred
    Tripped lightly to his trundle bed:
The tired hands and weary feet must rest,
While Santa Claus at midnight does his best
To fill the stockings with all they will hold
For little Freddie, the five-year-old.

O, bright and happy thoughts of days gone by!
Like rainbow colors that appear in sky
Enjoyed but a moment, then die out;
Our former expectations put to rout.
None but the child knew the gladness within
Or had the pleasure experienced by him.

When he was ten, " old Santa Claus " he knew;
Boys at school all said: " No such thing, 'twasn't
        true,
'Twas father and mother bought children things;
All of their handsome toys, sleds, dolls and rings."

He looked in cupboards, on the butt'ry shelf·
To find the presents they'd bought for himself.

He hurried to the Christmas tree at night,
Brim full of mischief, grinning left and right;
Spoke " Night Before Christmas," but had to stop,
In the midst of his piece his lines he forgot.
But the people spatted and jumped their feet
As Fred went to the aisle to take his seat.

At fifteen years of age they called him bad,
Though Fred was simply an over-grown lad;
Called " rough and lazy," and a " careless Turk"
Who'd rather hunt most any day than work:
He borrowed his brother's horse and sleigh
To take his girl out riding the next day.

When scarcely twenty Fred was deep in love
And called his sweetheart "pet," "dearie" and "dove."
They went to the "tree" in the highest style
And proudly walking up the long church aisle,
Took front seats in a conspicuous place,
Where each could see the other's smiling face

When Fred was about twenty-five years old,
Children were " teething " and his wife would scold ;
They didn't go a step to the Christmas tree,
To furnish a howling concert free,
But stayed at their home by the fireside bright
And rocked the children till far in the night.

Thirty years to Fred had now come about,
He and his wife looked hearty and stout ;
They bought for their two children, Ted and Nan,
Costly presents rare, and made ev'ry plan
For the bountiful time on Christmas Eve,
When all should be joyful with naught to grieve.

Thirty-five, forty years, 'twas much the same ;
Forty-five years, a double wedding came
To break the circle of the family home
And leave father and mother all alone :
Miss Nancy this Christmas Eve is a bride
And afar on a wedding tour will ride.

Ted tries his fortune in the distant west,
And is leaving the home that he loves best ;

While the merry company are glad with cheer,
Father and mother drop a silent tear;
And emotions strong that fill each sad heart,
Will choke down the words when they come to part.

Fifty years—Fred and wife are getting gray,
Children are coming home, now on the way;
The front rooms are lit up with greatest care
On Christmas Eve; glad hearts are everywhere:
The grandchildren climb up on grandpa's knee,
While he recites about the Christmas tree.

Fifty-five, sixty winters have rolled by:
Oh, how the days, months and years seem to fly!
The cheeks are hollow, and shrunken the skin;
Weak is the once strong frame, now old and thin;
The eyes are not bright as they used to be
At ten, when he spoke at the Christmas tree.

Some sixty-five years had passed over Fred
When his faithful wife lay on her death bed:
On Christmas Eve, when the world seemed so gay,
She was breathing her last and died next day.

Affliction's strong hand brought sorrow and gloom
To the poor old heart, so sadly and soon.

The bells are ringing at the Christmas tree;
Young hearts will beat with joy and happy glee:
Grandpa has reached his seventieth year;
The allotted time he has lived out here:
They try to wake him, raise the poor old head
But, alas! dear grandpa is cold and dead.

Children and grandchildren in five years meet
With a warm affection and welcome greet:
United family, good is their lot!
They've not disbanded, nor have they forgot
The Christmas Eve, with memories rife,
Made so by father and mother during life.

AFFLICTION.

A S comes a wind cloud, thick and dark
    Rolling o'er earth with a mighty sway,
Appalling the mind and the heart;
    So doth affliction in its day.

And, moving on with awful force,
    Appears no recess for escape ;
As roll the wide folds worse and worse,
    The soul sinks down to wait its fate.

On, on, the jet black lines unfold!
    Fierce the wild winds death-like roar!
Oh, agony, so great, untold!
    Will affliction hold forever more?

The lightning flashes streak out past,
    The thunder peals forth from its shroud
While heavy hail 'mid rain drops crash,
    Quaking the earth, the sky, and cloud.

Down, down, in sinking mind and soul
    The last sustaining hope goes out!
O, may Providence take control!
    Revive the hope, the heart make stout.

Now comes the infinite command
　　To tempest's fierce and roaring wrath:
" Stay, stay, thy cruel, wasting hand,
　　No right to kill, affliction hath ! "

" There's other work this soul must do;
　　I have a useful place for him ;
He shall to self henceforth be true;
　　I'll cleanse his heart from deadly sin."

The storm ceases, tempest is still,
　　The dense fog of affliction clears;
Winds and waves have obeyed His will,
　　Calmed and subdued are all the fears.

Then a peace, as when God is near,
　　Creeps softly o'er the sad, worn frame,
The tender heart forbears not a tear,
　　And heaven wipes away the same.

The drooping head by angels raised,
　　Looks up to heaven's righteous Son
And sings aloud:　" Now God be praised,
　　Affliction's o'er and I have won !"

I SAID, " FAREWELL."

I SAID " farewell " with tremulous voice,
   Fought back the inward feeling,
Tho' painful thoughts in heart and mind,
   Like drunken men, were reeling.

I said " farewell," I know 'tis true,
   Hard words had passed between us,
For fiery tongues and tempers too,
   Are ever ready for a fuss.

The idle words all uncontrolled,
   Like mighty floods went sweeping,
Tearing out bright friendship's ties
   While the inner soul was weeping.

I said " farewell," yet, fondly hoped
   That some day we'd both feel better ;
The outside nature easily ruffed,
   Would be held with an iron fetter.

When passion's storm had passed away,
   'Twas then we took a brighter view;

Resolved that vengeance would not pay,
That each his duty better do.

We met again, farewells were o'er
And the friends once more united,
Declared they'd quarrel never more
And their troubles thus were lighted.

Farewell no more, the trouble's o'er,
Shake hands, make up, be merry;
We're better friends than e'er before
And not so stubborn and contrary.

CRUMBS OF TRUTH.

LIKE some bright rosebud which unfolds its bloom,
  Developing rich colors and sweet perfume;
So let your lives good deeds, fond hopes, unfold
More precious than mere wealth of lands or gold.
May you, like heroes of the Trojan War,
Be read and known in distant lands afar;
Be it in war or peace where duty calls
Let your true banners float high o'er the walls;
A symbol of the victories you've won,
An honor to the land that calls you son.
Time shall point out the hour and name the day
When smiling fortune shall o'erspread your way;
He's found in workshops or in busy streets;
The slothful man he rarely sees or greets;
Though sought by all, he's but a cruel foe
When found by those who fail to feel or know
The value of his presence when he's near,
The awful loss when he shall disappear.

Ah, may your throbbing hearts ne'er feel the smite
Of cruel ingratitude and like that knight,

Firdausi, bard of ancient Persian fame,
Whose measured lines received a deathless name,
For he wrote sixty thousand couplets long,
The story of his native land in song;
And then, in sorrow he received—Oh, bitter thing!
The envy of a haughty, vicious king.
How true! we all are sinners more or less;
Facts are the same, but errors bad digress,
Mislead the fruitful mind, the heart, the soul;
We look at parts but fail to see the whole.
He that by admonition and good deeds,
Tries well to better life and help the needs
Of those about his way on ev'ry side;
Will find when stemming Jordan's mystic tide,
That all the loads of sin much lighter seem
When he recalls these in his dying dream.

Do not inscribe your sermons to the dead,
But rather to the living have them read;
Nor practice strange, incantation songs,
As did the old Egyptian, pagan, throngs;
For spirits, myths, and dead men's bones
Are seldom known to leave their proper homes,

But drink much at the fount of that queer maid
Whose four swift chargers white in air parade;
Who springs so quickly out from some high peak
And madly rushes down the incline steep;
Arrayed in flowing mantle of rich gold,
Her crown a hundred sparkling gems doth hold;
For she, strange figure of an ancient class,
The same that fills up Nectar's foaming glass.

Uncertain as the ways and life of man,
So is each thought; each confidential plan
Until it's tried by rigid, careful test
That'll prove the value of the good, the best.
When we attempt to view life's work complete,
'Tis like the mist o'er blue waters wide and deep;
The vast and wondrous sea of human thought
In which the problems of the day are wrought,
Scarce deigns to ripple when a small affair
Plunges 'neath its surface henceforth to share
The surging of its mighty rolling waves
Where all the world's great learning sways.

Can man so weak, full of conceptions wrong,
When evils spring up near and 'round him throng,

Search out, yea, fathom to the perfect right
Without a helper strong to aid his sight?
No, no, there must be had a royal chart
Whose maker knows the universe by heart;
A tested guide that's sure and cannot fail
When man's small bark 'mong shoals and rocks
    must sail;
Yea, when his spirit's tossed and thrown about
By overwhelming seas of fear and doubt;
He surely needs that steady, guiding Hand
To hold him up till he can reach the land.
O, boastful man, how small and vain you seem!
So proud, so inconsiderate and mean!
Not worthy of high heaven's loving care
Nor half the blessings which you daily share;
When will you change your hateful, wicked way
And to the Lord of Hosts due reverence pay?

Be there much at stake if he gain or lose,
Gross vice and sin must not inflame the muse
Of the fair singer's heart that sets on fire
The mind that governs life with love or ire;
For the true fire of eloquence and love

Is given to the poet from above;
He's but a clouded mirror that reflects
The works of art wherein his Lord directs.
He lifts his head to wait for lyric lays,
To catch some anthem sweet or song of praise
That only his listening soul can hear
When the vibrations are floating near.
Hark! now a beautiful, angelic theme
Awakes the muse as from a pleasant dream;
He glories in this blessed, happy state;
He loves his God, his home, and country great;
And hardly deems his poor, unworthy frame
Fit to repeat its Maker's holy name;
O, that lines could in some faint way express
The great sublimity of God's righteousness!

When youth has gone, with its aspiring mind,
Then, gray old age will come, at last we'll find
The goal of joy that we strived hard to gain,
Was but an empty dream whose thoughts were vain.
'Tis best to pause before we journey on
And consider what our hopes are built upon;
Lest crafty persiflage turn us aside

And we give over to false truths and pride.
Unscrupulous perversions ne'er will pay
The interest, on time lost in such a way;
So let us seek for truth, for wisdom, right,
Nor falter in the work, but in our might
Break down the dogmas that infest the land,
Uproot false theories on which men stand,
And then a happiness will come to us
If we've been faithful, to man been just;
Our contradistinction from the wrong
Will be recorded by the angel throng.

WORLDLY PLEASURE.

O COME, with worldly pleasure let us fill!
   While strains of music all our senses thrill;
While we remember naught but the gay world
In which the fashions of the time are whirled.
On with the dizzy dance, the gliding waltz;
To mirth be true, but to conscience false.
Now, join your hands with drunkards, thieves, and
      all;
Stop not with trifles, on with the merry ball!

Hurrah, boys! down to the pool-room gay,
"We're in for a time," "Real sport today";
Though disputes may arise about the game
And men with horrid oaths the place defame,
Deceivers lie in wait to take the last cent
Of the hard-earned wages, so meanly spent!
And fierce fights occur before it's done;
Stop not with trifles, go on with the fun!

"Here's to your health, boy, don't be afraid,
Drink up the bright wine ere its colors fade;
Oh, yes, my hearty, drink plenty, my lad;

'Tis time for pleasure, so away with the sad!"
Care not for troubles, burning sin and woe,
Or the drunkard's grave in which he'll go;
Though he's hung for crime in years to come,
Stop not with trifles, but on with the fun!

Let's have a merry sociable gay
And all the latest styles display;
Let ev'ry lady with her neighbors vie
To break the record and to dazzle the eye
With decorations in sumpt'ous array
And dress as only the wealthy may;
Of course, the poor have no business to come;
Don't halt o'er trifles, go on with the fun!

On Sunday morn, perhaps to church we'll go
Provided our seat's in a fashionable row
And we can listen to the birds of song
As they chant anthems that are loud and long.
The sermon's a lecture, a rhetorical affair
In which the people are unable to share,
Rich styles and dress shame the poor man's son;
Never mind such trifles, on with the fun!

The church that is most popular today
Is the one that has very little to say
Of the evils of life, the wicked man's way;
But speaks of our great men, the world at large,
Blind to the scripture's positive charge,
It preaches its members to heav'n away
Forgetting the fact of a Judgment Day;
Though they're preaching to please, and the "Word"
    they shun,
Why think of such trifles? on with the fun!

THE JUDGMENT.

Rev. 1-7: " Behold He cometh with clouds
And every eye shall see Him."

THE seven angels with their trumpets loud did
    sound
And hail with fire and blood, on earth came down!
Great clouds of smoke did black the sun and air;
A voice cried "Woe, Woe!" to sinners 'round:
Yet, they of all their evil ways repented not;
And when the seventh angel cast his vial
In air, full of the righteous wrath of God,
'Twas sounded out from the throne "'Tis done!"
No more by wicked ones shall earth be trod.

Behold, the lightning shines from east to west!
    The earth doth tremble and rock to and fro;
The mountains fall 'mid earthquake's awful roar!
    Men into dens and caves make haste to go:
But look! the heavens roll up as a scroll!
    The thick, black, rolling clouds change dazzling
        bright,
Lit up with awe-aspiring colors grand,
    Resplendent and sublime with holy light.

A mighty angel cries with lifted hand,
  Proclaims in awful tones o'er land and sea
To ev'ry living creature in the world
  That time has run its course and ceased to be;
Four angels standing on the doom'ed earth
  Hold fast the rushing winds that they blow not;
Dumb with amazement, prostrate, sick with fear,
  All eyes seem focussed on that brilliant spot
From whence the crashing, roaring thunders peal
  That break the rocks and shatter works of steel.

Hold now! a glittering cloud floats from the east!
  Ten thousand, thousand angels 'round it sing,
Ten thousand of his saints with him appear
  And all their ancient glory with them bring!
His throne is like a fiery flame of light;
  His chariot wheels are like a burning fire;
Before him spreads a crystal sea of glass
  On which the saints, the hosts that never tire,
Assemble to give praise and glory to his name,
  The righteous one, forevermore the same!

O, God! is this the Lamb whose blood was shed,
  Whose face outshines the noonday's brightest sun?

Is this the " King of Kings and Lord of Lords?"
  O, save us, save us, from the wrath to come!

The islands of the sea have fled away,
  The hills and mountains seem to melt like wax,
And saintly hosts in beauteous array
  Are gathering around the throne of God
To welcome on the Resurrection Day.
  The saints of God, so long in tombs asleep,
But now awake to everlasting joy
  No more to sorrow and no more to weep.

Hark! the solemn tones of the last trumpet sound!
  In but a moment's space—a short delay—
The faithful put on their immortal gowns
  And rise to meet the Savior high in air,
To rest with joy on that bright crystal sea
  And henceforth all his glory freely share:
The sea and land gave up their sleeping dead,
Their souls returned from whence in sleep they'd fled.

The wicked stand before the Judgment Seat,
  The books are opened and examined, read;
Alas! the search is made with tearful eye;

" Found wanting," the recording angel said:
O, God, I thought I had escaped from Thee!
  I thought that all was o'er when I was dead!
My wickedness, my shame, and all my wrong
  Laid bare before these saints and prophets old:
Can not the door of mercy ope' again?
  O, that I had heard what thy servants told!!

For holy work, thou didst not strive nor care;
  Thou art not fit to live with saintly bands;
Thou couldst not in their glory join or share;
  For satan did thy deeds in life control,
And won, yea justly claims thy wicked soul!

The mighty men cry bitterly and moan;
  And kings of earth call for the rocks to fall
To hide them from Him that sits upon the throne;
  The wicked fall upon their knees and cry:
" Thou art the Christ, the living son of God!
  Yea, it is just, that we should perish, die!!"

" Behold it is come, and it is done!"
" This is the day whereof I have spoken!"
The hour of the Lord's fierce anger is here;

For to avenge the prophet's holy blood;
To make the unbelieving tremble, fear;
To do away with satan and his works
And burn as chaff the place where evil lurks.

The world is stunned by earthquake's awful roar!
   And melts and burns as stubble with the heat;
Winds take the ashes and they're seen no more;
   But a new earth appears in view complete,
And the new heavens stretch far out in space!
O, glorious, divine! O, happy place!

SONGS TO " THE LAMB."

PART I.

SONG OF THE TWENTY-FOUR ELDERS.

We'll sing to Thee, our Lord,
　　Yea, thanks shall never end,
For holy is Thy word ;
　　To Thee our knees we bend.
Thou art most holy, just and true ;
Great is Thy might and blessing, too.

All glory is to Thee ;
　　On Thee, Great King we call,
For now Thy saints are free
　　In praise before Thee fall.
Thou art most worthy, Lord, to claim
A kingdom in Thine own great name.

Thy kingdom shall ne'er cease ;
　　Nor sorrows come again ;
But universal peace
　　Shall bless our fellow men ;
And all the tribes of men will see
In Christ, the one, who makes them free.

Take, Lord, our golden crowns,
　　We cast them at Thy feet;
In heav'n, Thy glory sounds;
　　On earth, Thy work's complete;
Thou didst Thy children all reclaim
And no more in their graves remain.

Thy face shines as the sun;
　　For righteous deeds are Thine;
Thou art God's only Son,
　　Most holy one divine:
Thou hast redeemed us by Thy blood
And saved us from sin's awful flood.

We give Thee thanks, O, God,
　　Which art and was to be;
Thou hast the billows trod
　　And calmed the angry sea:
O, Lord, we glorify Thy name
Because Thou art fore'er the same.

Let all the angels sing
　　Thy praise forevermore,

And saints their riches bring ;
   For they have much in store.
'Gainst those that have Thy works assailed,
O, Lamb of God, Thou hast prevailed!

PART II.

SONG OF THE ANGELS.

We'll strike the harps and sing -
   With holy music grand
Our songs with praise shall ring,
   For we are heaven's band.
O, God, Thy praise shall never cease;
All glory to the " Prince of Peace."

'Take now, the golden harps
   And touch their sacred strings;
The grandeur of the parts
   Resounds in sweetest rings,
Divinest strains in chorus bring :
O, hallelujah to the King!

Sing on, O, joyful souls,
   In measured accents sweet ;

We have no fun'ral tolls,
　　For men have ceased to sleep:
Let all the powers that 're above,
Sing of the great Redeemer's love.

O, glory to our King;
　　Adore the Master great
With hallelujahs, sing,
　　For this our happy state:
O, strike the mellow hearts of love,
All things are harmless as a dove.

To Thee, O, Lamb, most high,
　　Our songs shall ever be;
For we shall never sigh
　　Nor any trouble see;
But joy will crown all time to come,
Sing hallelujah to the Son.

O, make a joyful sound!
　　Sing of His might and grace
To all the hosts around,
　　And fill each holy place
With music from the sacred throng
Who've waited long to join our song.

Bright angels, chant on well,
    Fill heaven with your praise;
For man has risen that fell,
    And blest are all his ways:
Yea, sweetly sing your lyrics grand
To Christ, who stands at God's right hand.

PART III.

SONG OF THE MULTITUDE.

Before Thy throne we bow;
    All nations sing Thy praise;
We'll chant Thy glories now
    And bless Thee all our days.
O, sing, Redeemed, with loud acclaim
The grand and glorious refrain!

We shall not hunger more
    Nor ever thirsty be;
The Lamb will blessings pour
    As waters in the sea:
No night will come to mar our joy
Nor evil thoughts our souls annoy.

All tears He's wiped away,
 And wicked things are gone ;
The light of God's fair day
 Shines forth in early dawn :
O, Lord, how cheerful is our home !
No more in sorrow we shall roam.

Our hearts are Thine to keep
 Throughout eternity;
Thy mercy we'll repeat,
 But not adversity:
The skies with melodies resound,
The weary rest, the lost are found.

In adoration fall
 Before the mighty Prince ;
For Zion's harps, we'll call ;
 Again, they're playing, since
We've been redeemed and purified
And by the fire of God been tried.

O, holy, holy band !
 Our hearts in joy unite ;

We're in the Father's land
  In robes of purest white:
O, join our hymn, blest angels near
And sing "The New Song" that's so dear!

  O, chant the chorus grand!
    Let heaven's bells ring out!
  Thine is the glory, and,
    So now Thy people shout:
"O, alleluia to the Son!
Thrice ever blessed faithful One!"

TWO SONNETS.

IN MEMORY OF B. D. R.

No. 6.

O HAPPY hour when first we met as friends!
  Dear boy, how oft' my heart some message
    sends
To you once more again, but that is all.
No more we'll tramp the woods with sledge and mall
And hunt for shingle bolts to cut and sell,
Or draw the cross-cut saw and stories tell;
For earnest work caused us to leave our home,
Now, you are gone, and I still wander, roam.
Oh, then, we little thought 'twould thus be so!
Alas, of future things we do not know.
A Father's loving hand that's great and wise
Veils future sorrows from our earthly eyes;
For 'tis enough for us below to bear
The weary trials that each day we share.

No. 7.

Ah, comrade, friend of youthful bygone days,
In loving tones I sing these heartfelt lays;
For 'tis a morsel sweet, indeed, to think

Of some days that in life's chain form a link;
And we that comprehend the holy way
Will bless the loyal friendships of today.
Let's have more faithful hearts that ne'er will change,
That ne'er grow old with age and distant, strange;
For they will truly serve us much the best,
So firmly cling to them and you'll be blest.
When a forsaken world seems trying well,
To crush your hopes to ring your dying knell,
And darkest night shuts off the day from you,
What inward joy 'twill bring to know they're true!

SONNET NO. I.

I SING these lines to heaven's works so fair,
   I get them from the earth, the clouds and air;
I sing, for now my heart is flowing o'er
With love for God who's blessed forever more.
The fairy clouds which circle over head
Or form the background for the sunset red,
Imbue me now with God's most holy plan
Wherein the world, at first, was made for man.
And when I think of air, so pure, so good,
Of fertile land that gives to us our food,
Of roaring seas which give up treasures rare,
And mountains filled with riches which we share,
I bless the righteous hand that gave it all
And down before His throne in meekness fall.

A DIREFUL SONNET.

No. 3.

HOW strange! that men should use a harmful weed
And to their lives and health give little heed!
The dangers of this poison leaf are great;
Oft' old and young have found out, when too late,
That it takes life, takes strength, breaks down the nerves
And makes a slave of the poor man it serves.
In all its forms, no health or strength is found;
It blunts the nerves and makes the mind unsound;
The brighter thoughts give 'way to darker frown,
Caused by the weed which drags the creature down:
Their hearts that need to be so active, strong,
May fail and weaken by this awful wrong,
Then if great excesses have ruled, they die
And soon in early graves their forms will lie.

TWO SONNETS

TO YOUNG MEN.

No. 4.

DEAR boys, we meet you on the roads and streets
 And oft' at church receive your friendly greets;
We love you, but our hearts are often sad
To see bright youths with habits foul and bad.
Oh, how can you be good, and pure, and fair
When your breath with narcotics scents the air?
How can you meet your kind, good mother's face
When you are low, a shame and a disgrace?
Be valiant heroes of the human race,
Try not to be found in a wicked place;
Your companions in sin throw to one side;
Give up narcotics for your health and pride
Or, soon like raindrops from the clouds of God,
You'll be thrown with the trash, under the sod.

No. 5.

Fair boys, in morning's dawn of busy life,
How soon will come the world's sad cares and strife!
Weigh not your glad young hearts with useless care
Until life is a wreck and hopes despair:

Nor deem that life is a " Butterfly's Ball,"
Where showy colors must be worn by all :
Feel that an earnest work is to be done
And do not halt 'til the battle is won ;
For discouragements come that try the will
And you must o'ercome them with manly skill ;
Forgetting not that a great, mighty hand
Can guide you on to a much fairer land.
Young men and boys, be kind, be true and tried,
In years to come, be called the nation's pride.

THE IRON HORSE.

O LET me sing to the horse of steel !   .
    Though his iron heart no song can feel,
Perchance some friendly heart that's true
May hear my song and feel it, too ;
For marksmen bold oft' miss their aim
Yet, by this fault find greater game.

So powerfully strong you stand
That just a movement of the hand,
You gather up your forces well ;
You rush o'er plain, through leafy dell
And hasten along at a rapid rate
The progress in each growing state.   .

When on the straight and narrow road,
How smoothly onward moves your load !
Your wheels glide 'round in circles swift
And fiery cinders high upward drift ;
While all along your royal way
Your coming's hailed with joy each day.

But when you leave foundation strong
And pass o'er tot'ring bridges long,
Or madly rush 'round winding curves
Then fate gives what the act deserves :
All progress gone, your force is stopped,
Down by the roadside you are dropped.

HYMN.

No. 1.

HOW strong should be the Christian heart
    And always ready to do its part,
To follow out its Lord's command
And show God's power in the land;
To let the sparks of truth shine nigh
That all may live and none may die.

The straight and narrow road is sure,
Along its way the streams are pure;
No deadly germs infest the air,
But purity is everywhere;
The Lord himself directs the way
That leads into a perfect day.

The word of God is the solid rock
And worldly theories harm it not;
For Christian trains with mighty power
Pass 'long its highway ev'ry hour,
And carry with them God's elect,
Regardless of the world's neglect.

HYMN.

No. 2.

GREAT is our God, His mighty voice is heard
    Calling " Come back" to dear ones who have
   erred.
O, wonderful and infinitely grand
Are all His dealings with frail mortal man.

Sing to the Lord and rejoice in His name
Ring out o'er earth the beautiful refrain ;
For the Lord will bless each one's endeavor,
Christ is our king forever and ever.

Teach us, dear Father, how to live and do,
Incline our hearts to all Thy words so true ;
For ev'ry one that to the Cross will look,
Shall find his name in the great record book.

In Thee, O, Lord, I'll ever put my trust,
Thou hast prepared for all the pure and just
A home in Thy rich Kingdom where 'tis well,
There all Thy people shall forever dwell.

GRANDMA'S GRAVE.

IT seemed so sad and lonely
  When today I halted near
Where two years ago tomorrow
  Was buried grandma dear.

How can I express my feelings,
  How can I tell you now,
Of old-time memories that rushed
  So strangely to my brow?

I stand here by her grave,
  I talk, she cannot hear me now;
But the wind brings back the echo,
  O'er her grave, rose-bushes bow.

The pinks that 're on her grave,
  The birch sticks that are crossed;
Seem sadly to be reminding me
  Of the grandma I have lost.

I'm thinking, as I stand here,
  Of the many acts so kind
That she did here in her lifetime
  For those she's left behind.

Dear grandma, your battle here is o'er;
   But I'll meet you over there
When I have fought the fight
   And won forevermore.

But hush! she is sleeping now
   With a calm and sweet repose,
To rise with Christ, her Savior,
   When the Final Trumpet blows.

SWEET SLEEP OF THE DEAD.

HOW sweet the sleep of the silent dead!
　　Where's resting many a tired head,
Where many true hearts are still and cold,
Free from all sorrow and pain, we're told.

How sweet the sleep ot the silent dead!
When near their graves, pray lightly tread;
Disturb not their calm and peaceful sleep;
For those at rest, mourn not nor weep.

How sweet the sleep ot the silent dead!
While others toil on in their stead,
While the world doth war and volcanoes are gap'd,
They in unconscious sleep are wrapped.

They rest, yes, silently they sleep!
And angels' guard their watch will keep;
While lifeless bodies moulder 'way to dust;
As all mankind invariably must.

WHEN I LAY ME DOWN TO DIE.

THE sorrows, aches, and troubles
   That are mine in this short life;
I trust will all forgotten be
   When the tomb shall end the strife:
I'll pass away in joy without a sigh,
When I lay me down to die.

May the happy birds be singing
   In the air so light and free;
Let all of my friends be present,
   All of their faces I must see;
Let them smile and hush the cry,
When I lay me down to die.

Gather round my bedside softly,
   You, that are my friends so dear,
Sing a hymn quite low and gently;
   Let the music reach my ear.
Sing softly on as the moments fly,
When I lay me down to die.

DEATH.

O DEATH, how soon thy icy fingers come
    To pluck away our comrades one by one
And cast them downward to their earthly clay
There to await God's final judgment day.
We do not hear thy treacherous footstep soft
Nor feel thy awful presence with us near,
Until thy heavy shrouds have fallen down
And caught some merry friend, some loved one dear,
Ah, then, hearts ache, we see thee face to face;
Yes, you have come, O, enemy of our race!
How ruthlessly you tear them from our homes
And listen not, to our sad cries and groans.
They'll sleep for a time in an earthly tomb
There to await a triumph or a doom.
Sleep on, sleep on, in peace, O, fair ones rest!
O'er guarded by pure angels ever blest,
Until the Lord of Hosts shall come to claim
Those saintly ones that in the grave remain:
Their sleep will seem but a short rest from care,
Eternal glory they shall henceforth share.

WILL MY GRAVE NEGLECTED BE?

WHEN this life with me is ended
    And my face you cannot see,
When years have passed that I have slumbered;
    Tell me, shall I be forgotten,
Will my grave neglected be?

Will the earth that covers me o'er,
    Be grown to briars and to weeds?
Have I friends that will come ever
    To shed a loving tear o'er me,
Or will my grave neglected be?

Life is fleeting and uncertain,
    Troubles flock 'round thick and fast;
When death has set me free,
    Ah, shall I be remembered?
Oh, will my grave neglected be!

RIVER OF DEATH.

O GURGLING river swift, so dark and black,
How awful seems the surging of your waves!
And how we mourn o'er wrecks along your track ;
Poor barks! knew not the myst'ry of your ways.

Bring hither all the powerful lights, yea,
All of the scientific means of earth
And let us view this flood of moving clay;
Perchance we'll see the nature of our birth.

Alas! we cannot see through muddy streams,
The surface only to the eye appears
And all the rest's a fancy, as in dreams,
We stand in false positions, times, and years.

We know not what awaits us just ahead,
That's why we fear so oft' the unknown deep ;
We pause! we shudder! at thought of the dead
And we dread to think of the last long sleep.

What! must we cross the raging, stormy deep
Without a knowedge of the rocks below?

Can science or "chance-work" perform the feat
    And land us safely where we'd like to go?

There's only one true guide that knows the way;
    He'll make the angry waves calm and serene
And with his help some happy, future day
    We'll cross and view the glories now unseen.

MEMORIAL DAY.

WHAT means this sound of beating drums
   And church bell's solemn peal?
Where march these soldiers all in line
   With glittering guns of steel?

My son, it is the soldiers brave,
   The loyal men that saved our flag
In times of dangers vast and great,
   Who've come today to pay respect
   To those who shared less happier fate.

We've met to honor those who've fell,
   Who in the graveyard rest in sleep
And those in graves where none can tell;
   Angels their vigils o'er them'll keep;
   Today, America will weep.

'Tis not a day for loud hurrahs;
   Nor should we mirth and glee display;
We've met for patriotic cause,
   And 'tis a solemn, holy day
   Because of dear ones laid away.

Today the soldier's fife and drum
  Recalls the battle-field of old,
Brings back the glory that was won
  And thoughts of comrades still and cold:
  Our warriors brave!   Our warriors bold!

All people 'neath the flag unite
  To bless the boys who saved us when
Our foes would 've crushed us in their spite:
  America hath reared brave men
  As brave as any e'er have been.

The vet'rans left some day will hear
  The bugle's call no more below;
A few short years, we'll miss their cheer;
  Tott'ring footsteps and forms bent low
  Tell us too plainly they soon must go.

We'll deck the graves with flowers today,
  See that the flag on each one waves
While rustling leaves will seem to say:
  "Sleep on in peace most noble braves
  While we with garlands deck your graves."

They loved our country and their flag;
They fell in the fierce battle's roar;
Long as the Stars and Stripes shall wave
Their deeds of valor shall upward soar!
Honor to their names! forevermore.

EVENING SONG.

(To be read at the close of the day).

ONCE more the sun hath slipped away
   And twinkling lights appear;
The shining rays from restful moon
   All 'round are bright and clear.

The herds are resting on the hills
   'Mid bluegrass green and deep;
Afar on yonder farm is heard
   The call of some stray sheep.

The faithful dog lies near the door;
   And on the post near by,
The cat is purring sleepy tunes
   In answer to the hootowl's cry.

Old Speckle's brooding all her chicks
   Close by the dooryard gate;
The robin, in the large elm tree,
   Is chirping to his mate.

All nature seems to love her own,
    To cherish well her young ;
And he who studies out the art
    Can understand her tongue.

We cannot count the brilliant stars
    That're gleaming overhead ;
Nor can we view the unknown space
    Where all their paths have led.

We do not know when fate will say,
    " Your time has now gone by,
And all your future plans are naught;
    The *time* has come to die !"

So let us live that when our time
    Has run its course below,
That death shall have no terrors and
    We shall not fear to go.

Yes, let us live that our lives may
    Reach out to those around
And help the world, years after, we
    Are cold beneath the ground.

Much of the trouble of this life
  Could all be done away
If we could bring ourselves to see
  The blessings of today.

Too short, by far, our days are here
  For holding on to hate;
'Tis best to blot the thought clear out;
  Lest we receive like fate.

Religion's surely not an end;
  Nor learning's hall the goal;
It is the rescue of mankind,
  The saving of his soul.

Soon now, upon our beds, we'll lie;
  We know not when we'll rise;
It may not be until we meet
  Our Savior in the skies.

Again, pay to our God above,
  Around whose throne we'll meet:
" Care for us, Father, while we rest,
  Let angels guard our sleep."

THE GIFT.

THIS little gift accept of me,
   In memr'y let it dwell ;
In future days to come
   To you its truths 't will tell.

In weary hours or gloomy days,
   Read o'er the noble lines
Wrought out by men of honest birth
   With earnest hearts and minds.

Perhaps in some small nook among
   The poems of our time,
With trembling heart and bated breath,
   Some day, you'll read of mine.

BRIDGE OF INSPIRATION.

WHERE bends the road around the curve,
    The long bridge spans across the flat ;
'Neath it runs water fed by springs;
Near by the green frog croaks and sings
While leafy trees along the creek
Give charming shades that lovers seek.

Here matrons old and maidens young
Resort when mid-day's work is done ;
And many tales these pretty maids
Rehearse within the quiet shades
Of trees, which never, never, tell
  What's said inside the silent dell.

And oft' some gallant youth is seen
Making his way out to the green.
He's going out to view the park,
Perhaps his future wife to "spark ;"
And knowing not what else to say,
Talks on about a wedding day.

O, village boys, and village girls !
What does time bring as on he whirls ?

What joys has he in store for you
When each receives his own just due?
Oh, think, and act, that it may be
Blessings will come as floods from the sea.

On Sunday morn for inspiration,
Goes he who preaches of Salvation,
Out to the long bridge on the flat
To ponder over this and that,
To turn his sermon till it's done
In early morning's cheerful sun.

Then when his mind has soared to heights
Above the earth's dim, shallow lights;
Good things God always has in store,
And thoughts that never came before,
All come now, like a proclamation
Out by the Bridge of Inspiration.

Yes, it is well, a faithful token!
That pastors have with nature spoken;
For when we know of nature's plan,
We know the will of God to man;
Better for all of us to heed
The law of love than any creed.

TO A FRIEND.

WE live not for ourselves
        For nothing stands alone;
We're linked to other lives
    In school, in church, and home.

Let us then remember
    That others need our care;
Need a kind and gentle word
    When the heart is in despair.

For the morning of our lives
    Soon will pass and noon be here;
A little more of toil and strife
    Then the evening will appear.

O, well for you and me!
    When death's night settles down,
And still our hands upon our breast;
    If we have won the crown.

THE CREED.

(To a Lady).

TO you, most noble lady,
   These lines I will consign,
The thoughts expressed in simple verse
   If worthy of a moment's time
Note well, and kindly read
Precepts of friendship's creed.

I hold that they who love the good,
   Enjoy the beautiful,
As one that's great and noble should,
   Are always ones from which to choose
Our intimate, trusted friends,
Such ones as heaven sends.

They who despise not, nor scorn
   The music of the soul,
Some things that in the heart are born,
   Some thoughts beyond the heart's control,
These select from all the rest;
They will honor you the best.

Who loves his neighbor well,
  Does as the scriptures tell,
Who keeps his word at any cost,
  No matter what is gained or lost,
Deserves a worthy praise
As sung in grand majestic lays.

Beware how you do trust!
  The surface straws which float
About, and change their coat:
  Drifted 'round by a stormy sea,
These fair-day friends are found to be;
  Shun those who idly say
That friendships never pay.

Select those hearts that fear
  A silent thought or tear,
Unselfish, faithful, earnest souls;
  True till the last tie breaks that holds
Their life with ours on earth;
For great's their strength and worth.

DEATH OF A LITTLE BOY.

OH, little boy, so young!
   Yet pure as lily white,
We miss you, dearest one;
   No longer now in sight.

The sweet voice now is hushed;
   The playful hands are still;
Yet sorrow here we must;
   Since 'tis God's blessed will.

We left you, dear one, there;
   You're resting, sleeping, still;
Given o'er to angel's care
   Out on the graveyard hill.

Your little grave we'll deck
   With flowers bright and rare;
And think some day you'll beck
   Your parents over there.

O, weep not for the child!
   That was prepared to go;
In whom there was no guile
   And will meet the Savior so.

THERE IS ONE WHO HAS MY HEART.

A STRANGER wandered by one day;
  He seemed to have no friends at all—
No one that he could hope to win—
  And none his friend that he could call.
When asked if he in love had been,
  Replied: " In life we'll never part,
  Yes, there is one who has my heart.'

Yes, there is one who has my heart,
  In cares and sorrows always shares ;
That one will love me when I'm old,
  Will weep when I am still and cold:
I'm blessed through life till death shall part
That friend from me who has my heart.

There's always one that loves us best,
  Who listens with a willing ear
To all our trials great and small,
  Who stills each little doubt and fear ;
The one that saves us when we fall:
  A mother, wife, or other friend
  Stands by us till our life doth end.

Though all the world seems heedless, yet,
　There's always one who cares for us;
We may not know what heart it is;
　Some day a friend that's true and just,
Will brighten up our weariness:
　Then we with joyfulness can say,
　　" There's one who has my heart today."

CHRISTMAS SHOPPING.

A GAIN the merry, merry Christmas chimes
   Begin to ring out joyous, happy times:
      Frosty and cold the air
      With white snow ev'rywhere.
The sleigh bells jingle, jingle, 'long the road,
The foaming steeds prance with a jolly load.

Along the city streets in style they come;
In gay robes and bright feathers, now for fun!
      Dashing by the "slow pokes"
      And telling funny jokes.
They stop in front of some great bargain store
And over all the fancy treasures pore.

Some dainty little things to put away
That never can be used on any day,
      Are paid for, ordered sent
      To friends, who then give vent
In tones of great disgust, or much amused:
"Why didn't they send something that could be
   used?"

Now, honest Farmer Pete, on Christmas week,
Thinks best to market some of his spring wheat,
  Therefore begins to "quiz"
  His faithful helpmate, " Liz."
She says tonight the churning will be done
And they must start by the morrow's sun.

At eve, says Farmer Pete, " See to it, John,
That both of the new bridles are put on ;
  And ruffled hairs, my son,
  I must not find a one
On good old Fan and frisky old nag Tweed ;
Put in some hay, and corn, and oats, for feed."

The butter is churned, patted out in rolls,
" Liz" gets her brown dress down and smooths the
 folds,
  Mends quickly here and there
  Some broken stitch or tear.
The shawl that she's had since her wedding day
Is brought out from where it was put away.

Pete winds the clock, puts cats and dogs outside
And thinks of his trip and the long, cold ride :

Looks up his neckscarf red,
Sends Frank and Tom to bed,
Saying, " Your mother and I must get 'roun'
And early in the morning start for town."

Next morning just at four, both nags are fed,
The wheat and the butter put into the sled.
The steeds prance 'round and rear,
Keen is the frosty air;
But Pete and " Liz" care not for frost and cold
When the wheat and the butter must be sold.

"Our John must surely have a red necktie,
Or Jane Rose Stubbings may pass him by."
So muses " Liz" to Pete,
Sitting on the load of wheat.
"Frank's boots are old and worn out at the toes,
He needs some heavy ones to wade the snows."

Liz'beth must have a nice, new dress and hat,
Tommie a jumping jack, for he'll like that;
For Ann, a doll, let's see—
Oh, yes; candy for a tree.
Be sure to get some crackers and some cheese,
I'll heat the foot-stone so our feet won't freeze."

In town—show windows beautiful and bright,
Old Santa Claus seems ev'rywhere in sight.
  "Oh, ' Liz,' look, here's a bear!
  Ye—s, but just see—ah, there!"
Old Fan and Tweed jumped at the "stuffed affair,"
" Liz" mashed the butter that she had to spare.

Farmer Tom Gibbins meets his neighbor, Pete,
And asks the price of hogs, old corn and wheat
  Thinks we'll have a big storm,
  " The weather's been so warm."
" Liz" runs across the middle of the street
To give Sade Gibbins a warm, hearty greet.

All day the busy clerks must hurry, hurry!
'Mid great confusion and a constant worry:
  " How to do," " What's for you?"
  " Right this way's something new,"
Goods returned, ruined and spoiled, "didn't fit;"
People waiting, standing, no room to sit.

Pete and " Liz" prepare to start for home
And thus leave all the tired-out clerks alone.

The horses, Fan and Tweed,
Paw to go, "feel their feed."
At last the bundles are stored in the sleigh ;
Hurrah, they're ready now, for Christmas day!

ANOTHER DAY HAS FLED.

WITH setting sun a day has fled,
   'Tis past beyond recall;
It warns us that the day of death
   Soon comes to one and all.

And as the twilight deepens on,
   The shadows darker grow;
'Till all at once from out a cloud
   The moon's rays gently flow.

God's promises like moonbeams bless
   And throw lights 'round the soul;
They cheer us when we're in despair,
   When seas of sorrow roll.

Were it not for God's holy book,
   What would our wisdom be?
Or where, indeed, would mankind look
   For true security?

QUESTIONS.

T'ELL me, kind hearts, what's life ahead?
   What will they say when I am dead?
Will all the world rejoice and say,
" 'Tis better that he's passed away?"

Why do my friends oft' pass me by
And cause my heart to mourn and sigh?
Are they quite heedless of the care,
The sorrow which all souls must share?

What're my desires in days to come?
How many victories will then be won?
Oh, say! will all be lost to me,
My hopes all wrecked on a stormy sea?

Why do I scorn God's creatures here
And shun the souls so precious, dear?
Have I a different robe of flesh to wear
And so must not with others share?

Do I to God give thanks and praise
And honor justice in all my ways?
Will sad regret o'er these wasted years
Cause my life to end in bitter tears?

REVERIE BY MOONLIGHT.

MOONLIGHT ripples wave on gently
    In the balmy summer air,
Fancy's calling back my childhood
    And I sit in memory's chair.

Now I'm just a little fellow
    Playing, singing, all the day,
Mother's saying "Now my darling,
    Come and put your toys away."

Happy dream of early school days!
    Now the highest room is gained
Here the future's inspirations
  ˙ Led me on while I remained.

Now I'm with my comrade walking,
    He's a boy that's manly too,
Yes, we're planning for a party,
    Going with a jolly crew!

"All is gone and never'll come back"
    Says the wind with mournful sighs:
I wake, startled from my dreaming!
Each fond hope is broken, dies!

Oh! it must not be I'm waking:
    Surely that could never be!
All my comrades gone and left me,
    Youthful joys no more to see?

No, I will be young and happy
    While I live in years to come!
Age shall not mar golden pleasures
    Nor take 'way all my boyish fun!

Trees sigh, wave in gentle murmurs,
    Liquid rays of crystal light
Overcome my wild emotions
    And my dream's a future sight.

Standing near the crossroads, talking,
    Ah, I see my boyhood friends;
They have reached the place for choosing
    And should know where each road ends.

Some are careless and indifferent,
　　Knowing not what's on ahead ;
Only wasting precious moments,
　　Heeding not what friends have said.

Now, they're parted for life's journey;
　　Some have read the danger signs
And have taken royal pathways
　　With no crooks or faulty winds.

Oh, call them back!   Some are going
　　Where the lions watch by the way,
Glist'ning serpents charm their eyesight
　　And they'll fall an easy prey.

What is this?   My dim sight wavers!
　　Groaning creatures in despair!
Rolling in the filthy gutter,
　　Are my comrades once so fair !

"They are lost and gone for ever !"
　　Says the world with woeful pain :
"Always thought they'd end in trouble,
　　Let them suffer long the stain !"

No! no!   I love them yet, harsh world!
　　It shall not be as you have said!
I'll go trusting in the God of love
　　And bring them back to the Fountain head.

WAPSIPINICON SONG.

GLIDE, skaters, glide on the Wapsipinicon, ho!
    Glide, skaters, glide, the ice is free from snow!
    In merry rhyme our skates keep time,
    Hi l click'ty ho! now on we go l
    In joyous play, we sail away:
    Hurrah! for fun that's now begun!
    We'll beat the best and leave the rest
    To follow after, one by one.

Glide, skaters, glide on the Wapsipinicon, ho!
Let's all fall in, line up, get ready, go!!
    For frosty air we little care;
    The moon is bright, a lovely night!
    And the sport's nice on crystal ice:
    'Tis skaters run, look out! they come!
    They onward swoop and sing and whoop;
    This is the way to have your fun!

Glide, skaters, glide on the Wapsipinicon, ho!
Slip, slide, turn, glide, away, away we go!
    Now swiftly turn with quick discern
    And moving 'round with sudden bound,

Write out your name and date the same.
Glide in, glide out, the ice is stout:
To left, to right, a happy sight!
O, hear the friendly youngsters shout!

WE MAKE OUR FATE.

O THAT the young could now but dimly see
  The opportunities which are to be!
If they but knew the value of a day,
All energies would strive for learning's ray.

'Tis wasted hours, misspent and aimless years
That bring regrets and bitter, mournful tears.
Oh, wake them up! our coming generation;
For they must rule each powerful nation.

Boys and girls are just what they make themselves!
Honored, respected, and beloved, bright elves;
Or hated and despised by all their kin;
Because of ignorance, deep vice, and sin.

Men who have written books of rarest song,
Those who have ruled the world in vigor long,
Yea, all the great ones that have lived on earth,
Have made their own rich fortunes, fame and worth.

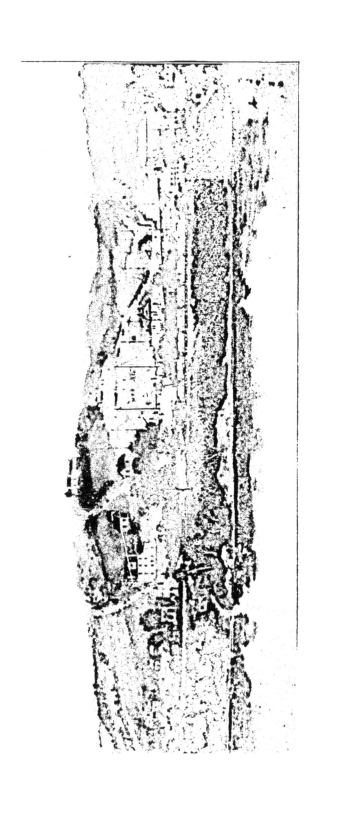

THE QUARRIES; OR, "FROM SUN TO SUN."

DEDICATED TO MY FRIENDS ON THE WAPSIPINICON.

I.

SUNRISE.

Where breaks the morning clear and cool,
    Soft breezes sighing over hills
Whose tops first catch the glist'ning sun
    That sparkles on the Wapsipinicon,
A wide river bending in its course
    Runs on in steady constant flow ;
Reminding us that we, like it, go
    On to our fate, our silent doom,
Drifting onward in a turbulent stream
    Oft' times awake, oft' times in a dream.
For tides wash out the shallow sand
    On which one's trembling feet doth stand,
Warns all to place them on solid rock
    Where rolling waves harm not the "flock,'

II.

NATURAL SCENERY.

O, grand is the scene from a hill-top's view!
    When rocks smile with June's latest flower,
And looking across from some high peak
    Houses and trees in the distance tower.
Here comes the seeker of nature's lesson
    To learn how she reigns supreme in the arts,
And to see the glow her magic imparts
    To far stretching landscape on Iowa soil;
For tourists who care not for trouble and toil,
    Will be amply rewarded by scenery fair,
Few places near that can compare.
    The oak and hickory's branching limbs,
Reaching far over the ledges' rims,
    Furnish a secure and convenient spot
For birds' nests to be bothered not.
    Here many a robin or bluejay chatters,
Not caring for the busy clatters
    Of the ceaseless shouting of men and boys,
The stone cutters adding to the noise,
    Or the steady chugging of Channeler drill

The clanging of tools of finest steel ;
    Nor will they stop one note of song
At the sound of bell or dinner gong.

III.

MAJESTY OF GOD AND NATURE.

O frail, indeed, is mortal man !
    He knows it when his eyes doth scan
The mighty hills, the valleys deep,
    The great stone ledges sharp and steep.
Who has conceived the stupendous plan
    Of shaping mountains, rocks and sand ?
We see our maker in everything
    E'en as the echoes through the gorges ring.
And scenery grand which never dies
    But on the summits multiplies
Gives one a thrill of admiration
    Yes, God-like thoughts of inspiration.
Exquisite and fragrant nature's perfumes
    Rise o'er the hills, while merry birds' tunes
Fill the air as they circle around
    Above the hill tops far from the ground ;

Or in the low grass 'neath leafy shade
    Pour forth melodies in a serenade.

IV.

WILD FLOWERS AND VINES.

Pure odors rise and fill the air,
    And sweet the scent of the clover there,
The white heads pointing toward the sun
    While the eager, happy children run
To find the four-leaf lucky stem
    Which always means so much to them.
And mandrakes blooming under cover
    Of long grapevines, whose strong scents hover
About and make the woods so sweet out door
    That one could wish for it evermore.
Twining and climbing on tree-tops tall
    The grapevines hang up over all.
Wild flowers beautiful and rare
    Hold up their heads in the pleasant air.
The blackberry's snowflake blossoms dot
    Each cottage lane and garden spot.
All nature here seems trying her best
    To far out-rival all the rest.

V.

THE TOWN AND QUARRIES.

When strangers inquire for the town
    'Tis pointed out on the hills around:
For nestling closely in cozy shade,
    Or near the ledge's rugged glade,
The workmen's homes so bright and free
    Far as the eye has power to see
Dot the hills and valleys afar
    And shine at night like the evening star.
When nearing town from an eastern side
    Through rocks and quarries the train doth glide,
Then dashing out in an open space
    A large store meets the engine's face.
In a half-circle to the right
    Great stone ledges appear in sight.
The tank and bridges on the river
    As trains pass over shake and quiver.
The word "Columbia" meets the eye
    In the sunlight on a building high;
This structure as a monument stands
    Erected by the workmen's hands,

Taken out of the solid rock
　　It stands secure 'gainst any shock
Of raging storm, or tempest blow,
　　And will stand as years come and go.

VI.

THE TOWN AND QUARRIES.

High on an elevation rests
　　A handsome dwelling, one of the best,
The means and material that form its worth
　　Were taken out of the fertile earth,
For out of the earth men of the place
　　Their property and values trace.
And farther on to greet your eye
　　On either side more quarries lie.
A winding brook meets you here
　　Speeding on to the river near.
Overhanging rocks shade the path
　　And save from an untimely bath
People traveling to the store,
　　Caught in a thunder shower's pour.

The old mill-dam, near by the mill,
   Save the rippling of water, all is still;
Years ago it ground out the grist
   Now it 's mouldering in the foggy mist.

VII.

COMMENCEMENT OF THE DAY'S WORK.

When the morning bell·gives out its call
   The men and boys, both large and small,
Commence the daily, weary task,
   Sometimes with heavy powder blast
To break the solid rocks apart
   And give the workmen a better start.
Then click, click, steel strikes the stone,
   The derricks swing 'round, the cables groan,
The lazy horse winds up the thread
   Until the stone is high in the sled;
Then swinging the boat o'er truck or car
   The stone falls down with a heavy jar.
And oftentimes the workman's hurt
   By caving in of rocks and dirt;

Lame shoulders, bruised hands and feet,
    Are every day the laborer's treat.
Thus the early hours are passed in work,
    The foreman shouting to those who shirk.

VIII.

SCHOOL WORK.

Teachers and pupils stroll on. to school
    In the early morning while it 's cool;
Many a subject, sad, solemn, or gay,
    Is discussed with energy upon the way.
Oft' the master walking alone,
    From school returning to his home,
Ponders over his work with care,
    Notes the advancement everywhere,
Battle 'gainst it hard as he may
    He sees the failures of the day.
But when he thinks of life at best
    Disappointment leads all the rest,
Like bubbles blown in happy glee
    ' Glide up, and soon will broken be;

So our fond hopes in life doth seem
  To pass 'way like a midnight dream,
Yet, when ambition's shining star
  Glows brightly 'cross our path afar,
We brush our troubles all aside
  Renew our efforts to stem the tide.

IX.

CLOSE OF THE DAY'S WORK.

At the joyful hour when sun declines,
  Falls back behind the brush and vines,
The quarry-bell chimes in joyous tones,.
  Long lines of workmen go to their homes
Traveling up long, steep, stony roads ;
  Some cheerful, others in gloomy moods,
Hungry and tired, but soon they 'll rest
  Happy with those who love them best.
Then when cool evening's balmly breeze
  Sighs sleepily 'mong the verdant trees,
The whip-poor-will on some distant log
  Sings his notes in the gathering fog.

Just where the waters ripple, glide,
　　There jumps the fish with sparkling side:
Right in the bend of the river, hark !
　　There comes a shout from the base-ball park.

X.

RECREATIONS.

Around the station at evening tide
　　The boys, who near the town reside,
Come out to have their sport and play
　　After the hard labors of the day.
They jump, throw—as athletes vie,
　　To beat the town boys, hard they try.
After the mail is given about
　　And the lights are all put out,
The stories stop, the boys go home,
　　Sometimes in crowds, sometimes alone.
Now all is quiet save here and there
　　The night-hawk dips in the summer air ;
And the watch-dog gives a mournful howl
　　Answering the distant hooting owl.

The moon looks down with its solemn face
    As if trying to picture or to trace
The rocks and scenery that 're near by
    On some feathery cloud in the distant sky.

XI.

DREAMS.

The slumbering town dreams on
    Of future days that 're yet to come.
Each cottager will own his place,
    His wife's best gown be trimmed with lace,
His children all to high school go
    And ne'er be counted with the low.
Of contracts great the quarryman dreams
    Everybody just now it seems
Wants stone for bridges, walls and houses;
    In the hurry he 'most arouses.
Then settling down to sleep again
    He dreams his men so good have been
He'll give them each an extra day
    And add a dollar to their pay.

Now comes a sound, refreshing sleep,
  To weary souls 't is good and sweet,
For the tired brain gets needful rest
  When Morpheus hovers o'er the nest,
Like a mother-bird when danger 's near
  Flies swiftly to her loved ones dear,
So God doth send His angels down
  To breathe His spirit all around
Among His people here below
  As to and fro in earth they go.

XII.

FROM MIDNIGHT TILL SUNRISE.

Calm is the midnight hour and still
  Only the rippling of some brook or rill
Disturbs the quiet serene repose
  As over eddies and rocks it flows
The gray, cold stone reflects the light
  Of the moon's pale beams in the silent night,
While stars that twinkle all alone
  Look down upon the piles of stone.

The plants and trees on dew-drops feast
  'Till Old Sol rises in the east,
Then moon and stars all disappear
  For radiant light again is here.

A BOY'S DUTY.

O FICKLE boy, despise not good
　　In early youth and manhood prime!
Remember what the wise man said:
　　There 'll come a final reck'ning time.

Think not, O boy, in merry glee,
　　That you have nothing left to do:
"For youth is the time to serve the Lord"
　　And the Lord requireth it from you.

"Despise not holy things," 'tis said,
　　By Him who holds your life in trust:
For hymns and prayers oft have led
　　The soul to seek the Father, just.

So be not careless in God's work,
　　But stand a valiant hero tried;
If you would reap the Great Reward
　　And with the saints at last abide.

SONG.

WE love the kind hearts of our friends,
  Those who regard the laws of right,
Who strive to live "The Golden Rule"
  Each day within their Maker's sight.

The angels bright rejoice to fall
  Before the throne of God on high,
To follow out His great commands
  Beneath His ever watchful eye.

Then let us think the purest thoughts
  And do our best in kindest deeds ;
For better lives with grander hopes
  Are what the world at present needs.

INTELLECTUAL SOCIETIES.

O MIND of mortal beings, thou dost tread
    Where angels in their beamy flight are wont
To pause and listen to thy cares and joys!
None but the messengers of God can grasp
The secrets which thou hast concealed within,
Or fathom to the depths where thou hast been
In midnight wanderings with self alone.

When companies of spiritual thoughts
Assemble 'round thy dwelling place to bring
Estrangement cold between thy soul and earth,
The glories unrevealed are brought to view;
And through the curtained windows of the soul,
A better life is seen just on beyond.

The cultivation of the mind requires
A systematic placing of ideas
That come and go like mystic spirits from
A far off world of thought that's unexplored.
The brilliant dreams of life flit 'way unseen,
While only stragglers of a small degree
Are caught in meshes of the inky pen.

'Tis inner thoughts and not our words that tell
The past and future story of our lives;
Words are but erring servants of the mind
Unable to transmit the complex scenes
Of human life filled up with joyous hopes,
Or darkened by unfortunate despair.

The objurgations heaped upon our friends
That fall so heav'ly on their hearts, are caused
By misinterpretations of their thoughts
And fatal willingness upon our part
To see the darker side of petty wrongs.

To have a predilection of your own
For certain rules of form and etiquette
Not found in formal books designed to tell
The proper things society demands,
Is to bring imprecations on your head,
To be misjudged by many of your kin,
And scolded by a frowning world because
The inward nature will not stoop and bend
To baneful follies that infest the groups
Of literary dens whose mission is,
To light the universal home of thought.

Book culture is to thinking minds, a feast
Enjoyed for its mental strength and light,
What food is to the body's urgent needs
When taken at the proper time and place
And chosen from substantial meats and grains.
Too much book lore is worse than none; for then
The whole is lost, and weakness comes to rent
The vacant halls where wisdom lately dwelt.

Some incorporeal currents that control
The pen, are not quite understood by those
Who ransack through an author's book to find
The key of secret thoughts and thus unlock
Forbidden rooms to gratify their whims,
Or satisfy a base and selfish end.

O erring mortals, how can you divulge
The secrets which alone belong to God?
Have you been granted leave to peer within
The sacred temple of the living God?
Then let your vain imaginations cease,
Learn that which was intended to be known
And waste not precious hours in fruitless search

For things which heaven will surely bring to light
When proper reasons for their use appear.

Ah, note the selfishness that fills the hearts
Of human souls who tread the walks of life !
Each for himself would praise and glory get.
And after that, perhaps he 'll tolerate
Some little credit to his vanquished foes,
Who were his rivals in the worldly marts
Where power wins regardless of the way
In which the potent strength has been acquired.

Societies should have their proper place
Which is to elevate the noble hearts
That God has placed within the breasts of men ;
To bring about a pure and righteous life
So Paradise may open wide its doors
And gladly let the weary pilgrims in,
To join in everlasting songs of praise
And live in peace where joy forever reigns.

DIVINE MUSIC.

O MUSIC, how it stirs the soul!
      Arouses all that's good and true;
It touches chords beyond control
And brings fair heaven so very near
That we can feel and know its charm
And live in peace secure from harm.

Celestial glories hover 'round;
The air is fragrant with their breath,
And teeming with the magic sound
Of instruments divinely played
By skillful hands with masters' art
So thrilling to the human heart!

O, lead me to the fountain head!
Where music flows in constant streams;
There let this longing heart be fed
With lyrics from the ancients' dreams;
Then gloomy night will fly away
And joy will bring a cheerful ray.

THE LAKE.

SPARKLE and shine, O, lake of the forest!
 Gayly your waters dash up their white spray;
Naught but light breezes can touch your clear waves;
No evil tempest in here ever raves.

Plainly the clouds upon thee are mirrored,
Darkly their shadows creep over thy face;
The waterfowl comes to recline on your breast;
Here is the haven of seclusion and rest.

Weary and careworn with life's cares hanging,
Swinging like branches torn by the winds,
We come to the lake for a peaceful rest,
And to stay for a while as nature's guest.

O, how refreshed are the drooping spirits!
Life seems worth living and cares are all gone;
Home then returning with renewed courage strong,
Our hearts are lighter, our lips breathe a song.

CLOSING ODES.

ODE I.

O CHANGEFUL world, take this, my book,
    Your judgment I must bear;
So meekly let your critics scan,
    And of their faults beware.

I fain would gather up my thoughts,
    Poor children of my brain,
And place them in a hidden vault
    Where none could see again.

'Twould not be brave to falter now,
    To shrink from public gaze;
For others have this trial borne
    And died without your praise.

ODE II.

We measure out excessive cares,
    When fashion's rigid forms decide
The doubtful questions of our life;
    And sense is humbled low through pride.

Yet, pride 's consistent in its place,
    Deserves a candid hearing when
We sit in judgment to define
    The rights and privileges of men.

'Tis pride that stimulates the young
    When slothful thoughts would interfere,
And crush the energetic plans,
    Or stay their progress year by year.

ODE III.

An apothegm may cause some one to pause
That's speeding headlong on a doubtful road;
May change the ebullition to a cause
Quite worthy of a tender, human soul
That feels a lofty sentiment condole.

The feelings of an earnest mind will rise
Within their covered walls and cushioned cells,
And longing for a broader field, devise
Some way to reach the outer world of life
And mingle in its pleasure and its strife.

The silken bands that bind the soul's desire,
Are loosened from their tightened folds
When noble thoughts of truth and right aspire
To reach a wider plain and help along
Our fellow trav'lers in the passing throng.

ODE IV.

Know this: That when the fog of life has cleared
    away
And intellects are broadened by the light of day,
That vengeful spirits of the earth will disappear,
In order that meek souls may long inhabit here.

CPSIA information can be obtained
at www.ICGtesting.com
Printed in the USA
BVHW042315290119
539019BV00010B/135/P